The Adoption
Reunion Handbook

be

or

The Adoption Reunion Handbook

LIZ TRINDER
University of East Anglia, UK

JULIA FEAST
British Association for Adoption and Fostering, London, UK

DAVID HOWE
University of East Anglia, UK

John Wiley & Sons, Ltd

Other Wiley Editorial Offices

John Wiley & Sons Inc., 111 River Street, Hoboken, NJ 07030, USA

Jossey-Bass, 989 Market Street, San Francisco, CA 94103-1741, USA

Wiley-VCH Verlag GmbH, Boschstr. 12, D-69469 Weinheim, Germany

John Wiley & Sons Australia Ltd, 33 Park Road, Milton, Queensland 4064, Australia

John Wiley & Sons (Asia) Pte Ltd, 2 Clementi Loop #02-01, Jin Xing Distripark, Singapore 129809

John Wiley & Sons Canada Ltd, 22 Worcester Road, Etobicoke, Ontario, Canada M9W 1L1

Wiley also publishes its books in a variety of electronic formats. Some content that appears in print
may not be available in electronic books.

Library of Congress Cataloging-in-Publication Data

Trinder, Liz.
        The adoption reunion handbook / Liz Trinder, Julia Feast, David Howe.
          p.   cm.
        Includes bibliographical references and index.
        ISBN 0-470-09422-2 (pbk. : alk. paper)
1. Adoptees – Great Britain – Identification – Handbooks, manuals, etc.
2. Birthparents – Great Britain—Identification – Handbooks, manuals, etc.
3. Public records – Great Britain – Handbooks, manuals, etc.
4. Adoption – Great Britain – Psychological aspects.   I. Feast, Julia.   II. Howe, David, 1946–
III. Title.
    HV875.58.G7 T74 2004
    362.82'98 – dc22

                                                                                    2004004225

British Library Cataloguing in Publication Data
A catalogue record for this book is available from the British Library

ISBN 0-470-09422-2

Typeset in 9.5/13pt Photina by SNP Best-set Typesetter Ltd., Hong Kong
Printed and bound in Great Britain by TJ International Ltd, Padstow, Cornwall
This book is printed on acid-free paper responsibly manufactured from sustainable forestry
in which at least two trees are planted for each one used for paper production.

Contents

About the authors

DR LIZ TRINDER is a researcher into family relationships. Most of her work is in the area of contact after divorce, e.g. the recent report for the Joseph Rowntree Foundation on *Making Contact*. This is the first time she has written about adoption. She was herself adopted.

JULIA FEAST currently works at the British Association of Adoption and Fostering (BAAF), London, as the Policy, Research and Development Consultant. In the past she managed the post-adoption and care counselling research project, The Children's Society and has counselled a number of people who have been adopted and also those who were brought up in Care through the search and reunion process. She has published many articles on the subject of Adoption Search and Reunion and also the information needs of children conceived as a result of donor-assisted conception. She is co-author of *Preparing for Reunion: Experiences from the Adoption Circle* (The Children's Society, 1994; new edition 1998) and *Adoption, Search and Reunion: The Long-Term Experience of Adopted Adults* (The Children's Society, 2000; now published by BAAF), and *Searching Questions: Origins, Identity and Adoption* (BAAF, 2003).

DR DAVID HOWE has a long-standing interest in all aspects of adoption. He is the author of many books, including *Half a Million Women: Mothers who Lose their Children by Adoption* (Penguin), *Adopters on Adoption* (BAAF), *Patterns of Adoption: Nature, Nurture and Psychosocial Development* (Blackwell Science), and, with Julia Feast, *Adoption, Search and Reunion: The Long-Term Experience of Adopted Adults* (The Children's Society, 2000; now published by BAAF).

Preface

When I agreed to be the lead author on this book I never anticipated quite how long it would take or what a personal impact it would have on me. Writing this book has been a revelation and a personal journey. As an adopted person, I had never been particularly interested in my birth family and had always identified strongly with my adoptive family. I joined the School of Social Work at the University of East Anglia to do research on divorce and separation. It was only later that I learned that a major study on adoption search and reunion was being carried out in the School with The Children's Society. Hearing about the findings of the study was the first time that I had really started to think about adoption. One of the things that rattled me was the use of intermediary services enabling birth relatives to make contact with adopted people. I hadn't known that that was possible and wrote an article criticising the practice and arguing in favour of using the Adoption Contact Register (where both adopted people and birth relatives can sign up independently and can then be matched). It was the first time that I had written anything about adoption.

At that point, although I was not interested in my own background (or didn't think I was), something was drawing me in. The main part of the Adoption Search and Reunion study had been completed but there were still 74 long interviews with adopted adults that had not been fully analysed. I volunteered. That was when my own roller-coaster ride began. The interviews were sent to me in four batches. I remember reading them all day and all night. The stories included joyous reunions, rejections, adopted people who were angry at being contacted, stormy reunions and people who had searched and were thinking about reunion. I felt overwhelmed, sometimes shocked, sometimes fascinated, sometimes cheering people on. Sometimes thinking 'Yes, I've got to do it' and then thinking 'God, no way would I risk that'.

What really struck home, however, was reading the interview statements of people who had been angry at being approached by The Children's Society Intermediary Service on behalf of a birth relative. Many of the things that they said confirmed what I had thought – that plenty of adopted people are simply not interested in their birth families and feel that their adoptive families are no different from any other type of family. What also hit me was the amount of energy that was being put into being not interested, almost protesting too much. That really made me think about where I was in all of this.

There began a long journey through the analysis and writing of this book. It has taken a lot longer than I had planned. At times I would have bursts of enthusiasm and the book would storm forward, then I would reach a difficult bit and find other things that seemed more important (or at least easier). It did not take me very long to realise that analysing the interviews and writing the book had a lot of parallels with the search and reunion process, with its ups and downs, turning points and false starts, usually with a lot of unexplored emotions lurking under the surface.

At times working on the book has been an absolute gift in helping me to work out what I think and feel about my own situation; at other times the material has just been too overwhelming. I also became conscious that although I felt I had a huge amount to learn from other people's experiences, I was also in danger of losing my objectivity or imposing my own thoughts and feelings on other people's stories. Although we have written this book as a team, and everything has always been checked out, I was the one doing most of the writing. At that point I decided to see a counsellor to get some perspective on what I wanted to do. I found it incredibly helpful in working out what I want and what my expectations might be. Although it wasn't the intention, it has also really freed up the process of writing the book, and let me see the interviews in a new light.

By writing this book I have learned a huge amount not only about adoption and reunion, but also about myself. Reading about the search and reunion pathways of others, and looking at my own process and motivations, has enabled me to call for my own adoption record and I know I shall make contact only if and when the time feels right. My message to you, the reader, is: 'You don't have to do this by yourself.' I hope this book will help you on the way. But if you can, try to get a mentor to help.

It is always traditional to thank interviewees in a research study as research cannot be done without people who are prepared to share their own experiences. For this study I want sincerely want to thank all the interviewees not just for their overwhelmingly honest contributions to the research, but also for what I have learned as both a researcher and a person. I hope that I have given something useful in return. I'd also like to thank my two colleagues, Julia and David, for being tolerant of my painstakingly slow progress. Many thanks, too, to my counsellor, Helen McLean, without whom this would have been a very different book. Finally I'd like to thank my parents for all the support they have given me on this journey.

Liz Trinder

Foreword

As one of the adopted people quoted in this book points out, 'If you . . . know where you're from in your history, you probably take it for granted.' Those of us who are adopted, however, have lost an entire family. Our roots, to a greater or lesser degree, remain a question mark during our formative years and often a lot longer.

It was during my own childhood when I worked out that the search for birth records – and in my case, birth relatives – is inevitably the only journey back into this past. Many years later, I made a further discovery – that it is not a journey ending with the reunion. As the American academic David Brodzinsky points out, adoption is a lifelong search because it is ultimately a search for self. 'Just as people don't mature once and then stay the same for the rest of their lives, they also don't wake up one day finished with thinking about adoption,' he says.

Despite the significance of the search in adopted people's lives, however, it is my experience – as well as those of many adopted people I have interviewed as a journalist – that its path can feel lonely, unguided and scary. There has long been help available but it can seem, at best, disparate and, at worst, inaccessible or impersonal.

Meanwhile, birth relatives – who, on various parts of the globe, are increasingly able to search for the people they have lost to adoption – can feel even more isolated and unsupported. Society has all too often treated them as invisible and without any real 'right' to trace birth relatives.

It is therefore with excitement that I welcome this book – a useful, systematic and highly detailed guide for people at all stages of the searching process. It is important not only for pulling together information and guidance on what is an emotionally and often practically complex journey – but also for incorporating candid accounts from ordinary people who have undergone their own individual searches.

These factors make this book all the more relevant to anyone who has an interest in, or is affected by, adoption. Indeed, the emotional ripples of searches and reunions can spread far and wide, with the people touched by them ranging from adoptive and birth relatives through to friends and partners.

Adoption is a unique blend of gains and losses, but the loss is less often acknowledged. This book is of great value in showing how search and reunion can help people come to terms with this loss. I only wish this book had been around when I did my own search. An essential and illuminating read for anyone involved in adoption reunion.

Kate Hilpern, journalist specialising in adoption

Acknowledgements

The origins of this book stretch back to a time when The Children's Society's Post Adoption and Care Project, based in Peckham, London, had already built up considerable experience working with adopted people interested in exploring their backgrounds, many of whom went on to have a reunion with one or more of their birth relatives. The project team was keen to have their work examined in greater depth. In particular, there was a lot of enthusiasm to look in more detail at what were the views of the many adopted people who had been helped by the project. The Nuffield Foundation was approached and agreed to fund a major study into adopted people's experiences of search and reunion. The findings have been reported in a variety of books and papers. However, it became increasingly apparent that what was also needed was a guide, a handbook, a how-to-do-it manual for all those adopted people thinking about a search, but still uncertain how to begin.

This book is the result of that recognition. It could not have been written without the support and help of a number of key people. The Peckham team of Denise Coster, Erica Peltier, Jenny Setterington, Janet Smith, Rose Wallace, Elizabeth Webb and Penny Whittingham put in a huge amount of effort at every stage of the project and we owe them many, many thanks. We are also extremely grateful for the support and backing of both The Children's Society and The Nuffield Foundation. Particular thanks must go to Sharon Witherspoon of The Nuffield Foundation who was a constant source of encouragement. And finally, we owe a big debt of gratitude to the hundreds of adopted people who shared their search and reunion stories with us. Their resilience and humour, thoughtfulness and sensitivity kept us captivated and engaged. Without their insights and openness the book would never have seen the light of day.

LT
JF
DH

Introduction

The search and reunion process is a leap into the
unknown for those involved and is likely to be a
rollercoaster ride of highs and lows.

Since the mid-1970s many Western countries have introduced new laws to enable adults
adopted as children to find out about and meet a birth relative. In other words to have
an 'adoption reunion'. More recently some countries, such as Australia, have also given
rights to birth relatives to make contact with the adopted person. In England and Wales,
the new Adoption and Children Act 2002 will mean that from 2005 birth relatives will
be able to ask an adoption support agency to make contact with the adopted person on
their behalf.

Ever since adoption reunions have been possible they have led to enormous public
interest and a lot of media coverage around the world. In the UK the reunion between
the former government minister Clare Short and her son was headline news. Search and
reunion have also figured strongly in magazine articles, film and soap opera plots and
TV shows like 'Kilroy' and 'Oprah Winfrey'.

One of the reasons why adoption reunions are such a favourite topic in the media is
that they are very dramatic and emotional. The search and reunion process is a leap into
the unknown for those involved. Whatever the outcome the search and reunion process
is likely to be a rollercoaster ride of highs and lows. For birth parents and children
meeting for the first time in decades, or siblings seeing each other for the very first time,
it is likely to be a highly charged process, often with high, sometimes unrealistic, expectations. But coverage of adoption reunions in the media does not necessarily give a clear
picture of what happens in the real world with real reunions. One of the distinctive fea-
tures of this book is that it is based on the real life experiences of a large number of people
who have actually gone through the search and reunion process. The authors were
involved in the largest UK research study of adoption search and reunion.[1] The study was
based on questionnaires completed by 394 adopted adults who had searched for information about birth relatives (the 'searchers') and 78 adopted adults who had been con-

---

[1] David Howe and Julia Feast (2000) *Adoption Search and Reunion: The Long-Term Experience of
Adopted Adults.* Originally published by The Children's Society, London, and now published
by BAAF, London (2004).

tacted by a birth relative (the 'non-searchers'). We followed up 74 of the questionnaire cases with an in-depth interview.

We have written this book as a guide for anyone who is thinking about undertaking a search and reunion and for those who are already involved in the process. We have been able to use our research findings to describe what *usually* happens in reunions, and the highs and lows to expect. We cannot, of course, predict what will happen in an individual reunion. As you read this book it will become clear that each reunion story is unique, with different people with different expectations in different circumstances. Even so, there are often common experiences that people can share and from which they can learn. There are no guarantees that a search and reunion will turn out exactly like those included here, but by describing what typically happens, as well as the sheer variety of reunions, we aim to help you to make your own decisions about whether to start your own search and reunion as well as to be as prepared as possible for the journey ahead. For those who have already embarked on the journey we hope the stories told here will give you insights to help you to negotiate and find your own way through some of the potential pitfalls and to get the support you might need. Although our research is based on reunions in the UK we are certain that many of the experiences, issues and emotions reported by our contributors will be just as relevant to people around the world.

The book also aims to give as much practical advice as possible. We include material, for example, on legal rights and on how to locate names and addresses of birth relatives. Chapters 2 and 3 describe the search process in England and Wales and the Appendix has information on searching in the rest of the UK, Ireland, Australia and New Zealand, Canada and the USA.

Most chapters also include 'advice boxes', summarising key points to bear in mind to make the search and reunion process as good as it can be; for example, advice on how to make initial contact and where/when to arrange a first meeting. Some of this advice comes from the adopted people themselves, others from our own collective experience. The Appendix contains an annotated list of further sources of advice and information. Some chapters also include worksheets that you may find helpful to work through when making decisions about the search and reunion process.

It is important to point out that we are not seeking to either encourage or discourage anyone from taking these steps. The overall message from our study is that search and reunion is usually an emotionally challenging process requiring a lot of consideration over the years, but one that most people are glad they began. Only you can decide if you are ready to take these steps. We hope that this book will help you to make these decisions and, if you decide to go ahead, to help you to be as prepared as possible.

A word about words

One of the many tricky aspects of writing this book is deciding what terms to use. Adoption reunion is one of those areas in which it is difficult to find terms that will be acceptable to everyone. The word 'reunion' itself will be unacceptable to some people who might feel uncomfortable with the implicit suggestion that there is an existing relationship that can be renewed. We use it simply because it is by now the most widely used and recognised term to describe the experience. There are similar problems with the term 'birth mother' or 'birth father'. Again we've chosen these as the most common terms but we know that other people would prefer 'natural' or 'blood' or 'biological' mother/father. We've also used 'adopted people' rather than 'adoptee'. We realise that this is a personal preference but adoptee to us denotes a category rather than a person.

Finally, we should point out that in this book we use many quotations from our research interviews with adopted people who have been through the search and reunion process. In order to preserve their anonymity, we have used substitute first names and place names throughout.

Taking the first step:
Birth record information

In this chapter we explain the practicalities of how
to go about getting a copy of your original birth certificate
and other information.

Introduction

Most adopted people think about their birth relatives during childhood and into adulthood, wondering what they might look like or what sort of people they were or are. Until
relatively recently finding answers to these questions was really difficult. Adopted people
had to rely on the limited information that their adoptive parents were able or willing to
share with them. In England and Wales[1] this situation changed in 1975 when you, as
an adopted person, were given the legal right to access information about your origins.
From that time you have been able to get a copy of your original birth certificate, with
your original name and birth mother's name. If your adoption was not a private arrangement, and you know or can find out the adoption agency that organised your adoption,
then it is usually possible for you to obtain information held on the adoption agency's
record. The amount of information can vary but usually the records will contain more
information about your birth parents and your family background.

You may well have already decided that you want to search for birth records information, and possibly have also made the decision to make contact with a birth relative.
We shall explain how you can obtain a copy of your original birth certificate and other
information held on the adoption record, either as an end in itself, or as the first step
towards making contact with a birth relative. Alternatively you might be at the start of
the process of thinking about searching. You know that it is possible but are wondering
whether it might be right for you. Only you can make this decision. To help you to think
about what might be right for you, we look at what other adopted people have said that
prompted them to search. We look at the kind of information that might be held in the
original birth and adoption records and the comments that people who have been
through the process say about what it was like for them.

In this chapter we look at the first stage of searching and reunion, that of making
the decision to get started (Advice Box). The next chapter covers the second and third
stages of tracing and making contact. Both chapters describe the process in England and

[1] See the Appendix for other Western countries.

Wales. If the adoption took place in Scotland, Northern Ireland, Republic of Ireland, Australia, New Zealand, Canada or the USA we suggest that you first look up the relevant section in the Appendix as this will give you a good idea of the relevant legal framework and adoption organisations. You should then take a look through the rest of this chapter and the next as both chapters have sections about making decisions on whether or not to search and seek a reunion and the experience of searching – all of which will be relevant to people residing outside England and Wales.

ADVICE BOX! ADVICE BOX! ADVICE BOX! ADVICE BOX! ADVICE BOX!

Outline of the stages and steps in searching and reunion

Getting birth records information

1. Making the decision to start the process.

2. Applying for access to obtain a copy of your original birth certificate and details of the agency that arranged the adoption.

3. Finding other information that may be held on adoption or court records.

Making the decision to start the process

Why might I want to get information?

Everyone has his or her own specific reasons for searching. From our research, three main issues kept coming up: roots, reasons and relationships. For the majority, the search was about wanting an answer to the question 'Where have I come from?'. In other words, needing to know about origins and roots. This might include wondering what birth parents looked like, and whether or not there are physical resemblances. It could include thinking about what sort of people they were and might be now, and whether the adopted person shares any of these traits. For adopted people of mixed parentage in particular, needing to know where they had come from, and so who they were, was an even more important issue.

Until relatively recently the model of adoption in the UK and most Western countries was a 'closed' one, based on the idea that all links with the birth family should be cut, with the adoptive family becoming to all intents and purposes just like any other family. In practice, however, things are not always so simple. Adopted people may feel very close to their adoptive parents and entirely comfortable in their adoptive family, but for most adopted people the mere fact of knowing that you have other genetically related parents leaves you wondering about them. Patrick, one of the interviewees in our study, explains how he gradually began to think more and more about his birth parents:

❝I think it's something, it's always with you I think. I was aware of being adopted but I didn't think about it, you just get on. But I think as you get older it becomes more of an issue, well for me it became more of an issue. I suppose I started to wonder the usual things like where I was from, you know what my parents were like, whether there were any diseases or stuff like that. It starts to become more of an issue I think as you get older and you begin to understand it more. . . . I remember thinking about my mum when I was 13/14 on my birthday, wondering what she's doing. And from then on as I got into my early twenties I started thinking about it a lot more. I wondered whether they were alive and if they were alive, you know where they were, and whether they looked like me, what they were doing, what the circumstances of the adoption were, you know the reasons for adoption. It's just a dark area if you like. It's like just not knowing about your beginnings. It's just a blank if you like, that part of your life and so you're starting from new. There's no information there. I think it's just human nature to want to know where you're from, so if you don't know where you're from, it's more of an issue. If you do know where you're from in your history, you probably take it for granted.❞

Patrick's experience is very typical. Like most adopted people he had known about his adoption from early childhood. In our research we found about three-quarters of people had been told about being adopted by the age of 5, and only 3 per cent had never been told by their parents that they had been adopted. For these 3 per cent they usually found out they were adopted by some other means, either being informed by another member of the family or coming across paper work by accident. Patrick continues to have a very warm and positive relationship with his adoptive parents and sister. However, his story is also typical in that, although his parents were very open about his adoption, it still remained a difficult and uncomfortable topic for everyone to talk about:

❝Ever since I can remember I've known I'm adopted. I mean I think my parents told me from a very, very early age, as soon as I could understand you know a little bit, you know obviously it's a build up isn't it over the years? When you're a child you don't know exactly what adoption means. I felt as though, yeah I think I probably felt free to ask questions, but I probably felt that I didn't want to. Do you know what I mean? There wasn't a ban on talking about it, but I just felt that it was probably a bit of an awkward subject and rather than just sort of . . . not rock the boat sort of thing. I don't mean literally, don't rock the boat, but I mean I didn't feel confident about asking. But it wasn't from my parents' point of view; it was probably from my own lack of confidence.❞

Patrick is not alone in having felt uncomfortable talking with his parents about the adoption. This was also the case for more than two-thirds of the people in our study. It is simply a difficult issue for adoptive families to talk about. Most adoptive parents did not have much information, but the unease about asking, and about telling, meant that over half of adopted people said that they had little or no information about their background. Some had only the barest details, possibly not even a name, although others had been given, or had found, copies of letters, the adoption papers or records.

As well as the interest in roots, the second issue that cropped up frequently was wanting to understand the *reasons* why the adoption had been necessary and what the circumstances had been. This interest in reasons could be simple curiosity or trying to make sense of the past. For some it reflected a strong sense of rejection, hurt and anger, as in Yasmin's case:

> 66At the end of the day she'd given me away once. I wanted to know why she gave me away – things like that, I wanted straight answers to my questions. 99

The third main reason for seeking information was a desire to make contact, or establish a relationship with a birth relative, particularly the birth mother. As Jacob says:

> 66I didn't go for information I went there to find contact. I wasn't really interested in the information – all I wanted was to meet someone. 99

When is the right time to search?

In England, Wales and Northern Ireland the earliest that adopted people may apply for a copy of their original birth certificate or adoption agency records is at age 18.[2] In practice, some people start their search as soon as they possibly can, although more people wait until their late twenties or early thirties.

For some people, of course, the time will never be right. We do not know the exact number of adopted people who actually search for information, although there are estimates that about half of adopted people search and half do not.

Some people never feel curious enough to want to search. Equally some people might want to search but are worried about what they might find, and so they delay, or never start a search. Another common concern is that the adoptive parents would feel hurt or angry by the decision to search, and this is dealt with in more detail in Chapter 7. Cora was one of those whose concern had made her delay a search:

> 66I was still going through that dilemma that adoptees go through with what effect will this have on my adoptive family and will I spoil my relationship with them for the rest of my life and therefore regret it. Obviously there were lots of other things that you consider like 'my natural mother might be mad, she might be dead' whatever, all those other things but that was the key one, that I didn't want my parents to feel that I was dissatisfied in any way with my life so far, or that they had been in any way lacking. 99

If you do decide to start a search it is so important that the time has to feel right for you. There may well not be a 'best' time, but the advice from many of our interviewees was to avoid doing the search during 'bad times' when things are difficult for you. However

---

[2] In Scotland it is 16 years, Australia 18 and New Zealand 20. See the Appendix for further details and for Ireland, Canada and the USA.

well the reunion might turn out, it is very likely to be a stressful journey with difficult challenges along the way.

It is important also to choose a time when you have support around you. This might be from family and friends or an adoption counsellor. The reason for stressing this is simple. Starting a search can be a nerve-wracking business, however keen you are to get on with it. The decision to get information is often likened to opening a Pandora's box where you do not know what might be found. People are concerned that the information about their birth relatives or the circumstances of the adoption might be upsetting. For Lawrence, it was simply the fear of the unknown:

> **"**My wife came along with me. It was a bit, how can you say it, like going to the dentist. You know, not knowing what was gonna happen, you know. Or going for an interview type-of-thing, it is, yeah, you didn't quite know what to expect.**"**

Getting birth records information is a major step. For most people the decision to search for information is not a one-off, snap decision. A typical pattern is to think and talk about the possibility of searching for information over the years or make tentative efforts to seek information until something finally triggers the final decision to take the next step. All sorts of issues might prompt that final decision to search: a TV programme about adoption, meeting other adopted people who have searched, the birth of a child, a new partner, a health scare, moving home, the death of an adoptive parent, or possibly a combination of different factors. For others it is simply about waiting until the time feels right, as it was for Jacob:

> **"**And I don't know why it was that I just woke up one morning and said 'this is the right time to do it'. And that was when I was about 25. I had been thinking about it more and more I think. Essentially I was waiting to feel . . . I've got an almost mystical belief in this 'right time' – I don't believe in thinking it through totally – I was just waiting for a feeling really. And I'm not quite sure what that feeling was and where it came from, but I knew I had it when I woke up one morning. Suddenly it felt comfortable in my head rather than conflict.**"**

For those of you who have made the decision to seek more information, or if you are curious about what might be involved, we now give a step-by-step guide to how you can obtain the information to find answers to some questions you may have, or to begin a search for your birth family.

Getting information: the original birth certificate

Once you have decided to get information about your family background, you have two potential steps to take. The first is to get a copy of your original birth certificate and the second is to contact the adoption agency that organised your adoption. You may already have your original birth certificate, and, if so, you can move straight to step two, accessing the adoption agency record. Most people, however, will have to start with step 1 as adopted people usually have only an adoption certificate or short birth certificate that gives the names of their adoptive parents. If this is the case for you, then you will need to get hold of the original birth certificate. This will give important information in its own right, but is also usually the first step towards getting access to the more extensive information found in the adoption record.

The original (pre-adoptive) birth certificate will include your original birth name, your birth mother's first name and maiden name (and married name if applicable) and her address at the time of registration. The birth father's name seldom appears, unless your birth parents were married or he gave his permission to be named on the birth certificate and attended the registrar's office when your birth was registered. If he is named, the certificate will also give his occupation.

Some adopted people already know their birth name, so it is simple to obtain a copy of this original birth certificate. You can apply for this via the Family Records Centre in London. The address is in the Appendix at the end of the book.

If, however, you do not know your original name then you will need to apply for access to your birth records under section 51 of the 1976 Adoption Act through the General Registrar's Office at the Office for National Statistics. You will need to write to the General Registrar explaining that you were adopted, giving your adopted name and your date of birth and they will be able to match this information with your original birth details. The Registrar General will not send the identifying information held on your original birth certificate directly to you. Instead, by law, it must be sent to an approved adoption counsellor at an agency of your choice and you will need to make an appointment for 'birth records counselling'. You can select your own agency. You could use your local social services department to receive this information (look them up under 'Adoption' in the phone book), or the adoption agency that arranged your adoption if you know which one it was, or a counsellor from the Office for National Statistics in Southport.

Some people feel puzzled, angry or upset that they are required to see a counsellor before getting access to what is, after all, personal information. The counselling appointment was originally included in the Adoption Act as up to that point birth and adoptive families had been told that no identifying information would ever be exchanged. The 'counselling' appointment gives you a chance to talk through with an experienced professional your hopes and expectations as well as the implications for yourself and for other people. You will also be able to get advice and information about any further steps you might want to take if, for example, you want to start a search for further information or birth relatives. The appointment is not intended to be a test, but is more a way of helping you to explore your options. We should point out that if you were adopted after 11 November 1975 then you can choose not to see a counsellor and instead have the information sent to you directly by post. This is up to you, but most people will probably find it helpful to have the opportunity to talk with someone with a lot of experience of the search and reunion process.

When you have met with the adoption counsellor you will receive a form that enables you to apply for your original birth certificate. You will also be given another form which you can send to the court where the adoption order was made. The court can then let you know the adoption agency that arranged your adoption so that you can contact them for further information about your family background and adoption.

Not all adoptions were arranged through a local authority or voluntary adoption agency. Some were arranged privately, for example, through the local doctor or local vicar. For people who were adopted privately it can be much more difficult to get information. In these situations it may be that the court record will have some background information. If you need to follow this route you should write to the clerk of the court where the adoption order was made. The clerk will be able to tell you whether or not it is possible to have access to this information and what you should do to get it. Sometimes an appointment is made for you to see a Judge who may then be able to answer some of the questions you have from the information held on the court record.

Getting information: the adoption records

Once you have the birth certificate, the next step is to get information held on the adoption agency's records. You will need to write to (or telephone) the adoption agency to ask for access to the information they hold. Normally an appointment would be made for you to see an adoption counsellor who will be able to go through the information with you.

The information held in an adoption record is likely to give you a lot more information than the birth certificate as there is usually information about birth family members. However, records do vary between a single page summary sheet or 30 or more pages depending upon the adoption agency, and providing that the records have been kept intact over the years.

During the past decade adoption agencies have become much more open and willing to share information that is held on their records. However, this does present some issues of confidentiality and rights to information. In general adoption agencies will usually give identifying, factual information to the adopted person, such as the birth parents' details and background to the adoption. It is usual for the adoption agency records to have recorded the name of the birth father if it is known.

The record could include information about the:

- Adopted person: e.g. original birth name, place of birth, weight at birth, brief medical notes. A copy of the original birth certificate is rarely included.
- Birth mother: including name, address at the time, physical and social characteristics, e.g. ethnicity, height, education and employment, family background including details of any other children. It could also include names, descriptions and addresses of other family members.
- Birth father: this is likely to be much less detailed or specific than information about the birth mother, and depends upon how much information the birth mother was prepared to disclose or if he was interviewed at the time of the adop-

tion. It should be pointed out that some adoption agencies will not disclose details about the birth father if he had not been interviewed as part of the adoption process.

- Adoptive parents: this may include the agency case notes and letters and reports on home circumstances.
- Circumstances/reason for the adoption: usually in the form of the adoption agency's case notes.
- Foster or other carers prior to the adoption: for people who were in care prior to adoption, there may well be much more information about this period, including medical information and possibly photographs.

In a few cases the record will also include more recent letters from the birth mother or father giving a current address if they have been in contact with the adoption agency.

What is the impact of having the information?

Sometimes people are taken by surprise about the feelings they experience when they see the information that is held by the adoption agency. You may be learning about lots of background information of which you were unaware before. For instance, you may learn that you already have a brother or sister or that you were looked after by your birth mother for several weeks. It is difficult to predict what the impact of getting this information will be. If you already have most, or all, of the information, then the impact might be quite limited. But if, like most of the people in our research, you have little existing information, then seeing the record for the first time is likely to make a much bigger impression, generating positive, negative, or mixed feelings.

The 'good things' that people in our research found from reading the record were listed as:

- Learned more about my birth mother.
- A better understanding of why I was adopted.
- Filled in gaps in information.
- Gained information to help with a search.
- Learned more about my birth father.
- Improved my sense of personal identity.

What this list doesn't show, however, is some of the emotional impact of the experience of reading the record or how unpredictable people's reactions can be to the information. David, for example, one of our interviewees, found getting the information an overwhelming, although positive, experience in a way that he had not anticipated:

> ❝It's difficult to comprehend the whole thing in one day really. I went home and I can't remember what upset me but I did go home and I did cry, for most of the evening.

And I don't cry very often at all. That's probably the only thing that's ever made me cry, except that and the Lassie films. So something in there must have. . . . I think it was all the information overload I think. All at once. As a child you imagine what she looks like, what she did, whether she's alive or she's dead, all sorts of things. But then to have someone sit down and say 'this is how you came about' and stuff like that. "

What can make reading the adoption record so powerful, as David points out, is that those who have to some extent been imaginary people suddenly come to life and become real for the first time. As Nina said 'I mean obviously I can't see them clearly but I've got my own little picture of what they look like.'

Perhaps the most profound impact is on people of mixed race who have the double question about who their parents are, and also what is their ethnicity. Una, who was adopted at 4 years of age and was now in her early forties, describes how the adoption record information enabled her to know for the first time her own ethnicity:

"I can remember when we found out that my father was Nigerian – I was sitting there, and my eyes just filled up with tears – she was Zimbabwean my friend, and it was always a joke that – just between the close friends that I had – that they were from the Caribbean and I didn't really know where . . . it just became a joke, it wasn't offensive or anything . . . but it just went 'you don't even know where you come from, so you just stay there, you can't say anything . . .' and then when I found that out – and we'd get into those kind of conversations again I'd be able to say 'well excuse me I'm the real thing, I am African! – you are one step removed – so . . .' (*both laugh*). You then had a retort to come back with – it was great, I thought it was wonderful – I really enjoyed those next few months – phoning everybody up and saying 'I'm the real thing . . .' – it was great (*both laugh*). Really excellent. Just because it places you – because even though you know that your mother is English and that you are mixed parentage – it still doesn't explain where your blackness comes from and that's what makes you whole then, when you actually know where that does come from. "

It is not always the factual details of names and dates that trigger the greatest reaction. For some people it is the small details that are important, giving more of a clue about birth parents and their feelings, than the official account might convey, often triggering feelings of sympathy, sometimes of anger. In our research 43 per cent of people said they felt more compassionate towards their birth mother. Elizabeth, for example, already had the basic details, but also learned much more about her birth mother from the small 'scraps' of information held in the record:

"It showed that I had been breast-fed and that I was with my birth mother for a couple of weeks I think. And going back on the train I think it had quite a profound effect really, because I think instead of just being a name on a piece of paper, I thought more deeply about her and having had the children fairly recently began to imagine what it must have been like for her to give up a baby. So I think it had quite a profound effect just that one fact, everything else I knew really. "

For other people, however, reading about the circumstances of the adoption can generate or fuel feelings of anger or rejection, as Ava commented:

> **❝**The counsellor told me what had happened, why I was put up for adoption, which was no surprise to me – of course she had a bastard daughter and she had to give her up. So what.**❞**

What information is difficult to hear?

For the majority of people reading the adoption record is a positive experience although it can be unsettling and overwhelming. Fortunately very few searchers have to deal with their worst fears of, for example, having been conceived as a result of rape or having birth parents who were involved in crime or a family history of mental illness. However, it is really important to be prepared for the difficult as well as the positive information.

In fact the most typical story in our research was that of the young unmarried mother who was not in the position to marry the father and who felt that she had little choice, given the times, other than to give up the child for adoption. Not surprisingly, these were the easiest stories to take on board.

However, not all stories involve mothers who appeared to have no alternatives available. One of the hardest things is to find yourself part of a larger sibling group where some children had been kept by the birth parents, but not others, or to find that the birth parents had subsequently married and had more children. This can lead to a sense of being singled out for rejection.

Even where the circumstances of the adoption were fairly straightforward, some of the contents or tone of the adoption record can still be upsetting or make you angry. Quite a few of our interviewees found it difficult to read about themselves as helpless infants that other people were making life-changing decisions about. Lawrence was upset at the tone of the adoption record and a sense of being treated almost like a commodity rather than a child:

> **❝**Reading the letter that says to my adoptive parents, 'we have this little one', they've called it, 'this little one', you know, 'would you like to come to see him and if he's acceptable to you, you can take him away that day'. That was a bit . . . And also there's another bit that says that you can keep it for three months, as if there's this guarantee. If the guarantee fails within three months you can give it back. If he's not acceptable we'll send him back; we'll go for another one.**❞**

Gail, another interviewee, was upset to find that the documents in her adoption record were headed 'Waifs & Strays', the former name of The Children's Society. She, like others, also was angry to see the actual piece of paper where her birth mother had signed her over for adoption, reinforcing feelings of rejection.

A health warning about adoption records

For most people it is likely that reading the adoption record will be a positive experience, giving a lot of new information and insight into your history and background. But we should stress, too, that the information recorded will have been gathered by social workers (or 'moral welfare' workers as many of them were called before the 1970s), probably reflecting the attitudes and values of a previous generation. This might mean that some of the material and language of the adoption record is more upsetting than it need be. There might be derogatory comments about the birth mother or father. People who are black or of mixed race may come across racist comments and unfounded judgements. It might also be the case that some of the interpretation of the facts, and even the 'facts' themselves, are misleading or plainly wrong.

Much of the adoption record will consist of reports or notes by social workers written at a time when attitudes towards single mothers were often judgemental and condemnatory. The birth mother may not agree with the account of the circumstances of the adoption or how she is described. The description and interpretation of the actions of the birth father may well also reflect the moral viewpoint of the social worker who had prepared the adoption record, and, perhaps, the feelings of the birth mother (usually birth fathers were not interviewed during the adoption process). In some cases it may be that the birth mother had deliberately withheld information or told untruths, particularly about the identity of the birth father – sometimes to protect herself, the birth father or the baby. Sometimes misleading or wrong information was given by the birth mother's parents who may have taken the main role in dealing with the adoption agency and organising the adoption.

Although the adoption records are 'official' documents it is worth approaching them with an open mind. In most cases the factual information will be accurate, but beyond that much of the interpretation, particularly of the reasons for the adoption, might well be just one view among many. They are not necessarily accurate portrayals of how either of your birth parents really felt about the situation or about you.

It's worth keeping an open mind in another respect. It is not just the social workers who were interpreting the 'facts' when they were putting together the adoption record. It's possible that your own interpretation of the information will be influenced by how you have felt or are feeling about the adoption. At one point you might feel angry at your birth mother, but on reading the adoption record again at a later date you might feel more sympathetic to her plight, or you might feel initially sympathetic to your birth father but later find your attitude hardening. It could be useful to talk through the information you have received from the adoption record with a number of different people. Lots of adopted people did this in our research, often wanting to share the information but also finding that other people came up with a different viewpoint which they could then think over. As one of our interviewees, Wendy, comments, it's important not to jump to conclusions:

> ❝I did feel that she'd [birth mother] had an awfully raw deal, but I think as I was thinking that I was saying 'this is quite a reaction, because you really don't know the full

story' – but it did seem to be very typical – a very typical situation: that she'd been abandoned by somebody. **"**

Final thoughts

Obtaining the information held on your original birth certificate, and any other information that may be held on the adoption agency's record, is a big step for most people. Only you can take this major decision. The items listed in the 'Summary' may help you to work through what is right for you; or, if you have already decided that you want to search, give some help on how to prepare yourself.

Summary

- Before setting out on a search for information try talking to a few people who are likely to have different opinions or have had different experiences. It may help in identifying the pros and cons as well as helping you to work out what your expectations, hopes and fears might be.

- Think about and write down on a piece of paper: What has led to you thinking about searching now? What are your expectations? What are you worried about? Who is available to support you through the process of getting the information?

- There is probably never a single *best* time to get the information, but there may well be a *worst* time. Our advice is to delay a search if you are feeling low and unsupported until things get better.

- Don't be pressured into looking for information. Only go ahead if and when you are ready for it. People are often very curious and enthusiastic about other people's searches, but they are not the people who are going to go through it. Equally if you want to go ahead, don't be put off if other people have a negative reaction – it is your search.

- If you do decide to go ahead, get as much support as you can in locating information and make sure that the help is going be available afterwards.

- Most people fear horror stories. This is very rare but it can occur and you will need to prepare for it. It is more likely, however, that the adoption record will be unsettling for other reasons – for example, possibly making you more aware of being rejected, or unsettling you as you learn that your birth mother may have been desperate to keep you but was totally unsupported.

Again, because of this possibility it is best to go ahead when life is feeling reasonably good.

- It may help to think about the search and reunion process in three separate steps: getting the information, locating birth relatives, and making contact. Some people will want to take all three steps and as quickly as they can. Other people will want to take all three steps but perhaps with months or years between them. Or taking step one or step two might be enough. It is your choice. The very best advice we can give is: Do what feels right for you.

- Finally, if you do obtain the adoption record, allow yourself enough time to let the material sink in, and remember that some of the contents may not necessarily be accurate.

On the search trail

Having obtained a copy of your original birth certificate and other information, you might be spurred on to begin an active search.

Introduction

In the previous chapter we looked at how to go about getting a copy of your original birth certificate and other information held by the adoption agency. Having found this information the next *possible* stage is to begin a search to locate birth relatives. As ever, we should stress that only you can decide if and when you want to proceed. You may decide not to go any further, at least at present, as you might be content with the amount of information you have. Or you may prefer to maintain the status quo and decide not to enter an unknown world of birth relatives and uncertain outcomes. Alternatively you might be spurred on by the information you have received and feel ready to take another step forward and begin an active search.

The main focus of this chapter is a step-by-step guide to carrying out the search for birth relatives. But it's important to think of the search phase as more than just a bit of detective work. It is likely to have a personal impact too and you will need to make decisions about searching or not searching, and if your search is successful what to do next. We start off the chapter by looking at what people said motivated them to move beyond the birth records information stage. We then move on to how to conduct the search before looking at people's experience of searching. If your adoption took place outside England and Wales we recommend that you check the relevant section of the Appendix before reading this chapter as the technical information on searching given here may be less helpful to you. The next section and the later sections entitled 'Life on the search trail' and 'Deciding whether or not to make contact' will be relevant to any search around the world.

To search or not to search?

Having obtained the original birth certificate and information held on the adoption record, the next big question is whether or not to take matters further. Some people decide that they want to search and make contact even before reading the adoption record, others only make their mind up afterwards. In our research, 85 per cent of people who received their birth records and adoption information then searched for a birth relative, and of those, 88 per cent had started their search within six months.

Although most people go on to search, it is not an automatic choice for everyone. The motivation for going ahead with the search again relates to roots, reasons and relationships. The birth certificate and adoption record will give some information about your family background and the circumstances surrounding the adoption, but for many people the information will not be enough or will not necessarily answer all questions. The adoption record information will help to build a general picture of the birth parents and the reasons for your adoption, but will not necessarily give all the details or help you to visualize them as they were then, and more particularly as they are now. As some of our interviewees pointed out, it was only by meeting birth relatives that the people described in the adoption record could become real. One interviewer, Eleanor, told us:

> ❝When I was 18 I applied for the information that was around my birth, but then I decided not to do anything about searching. That had sorted out that immediate crisis – about who I was and where I came from – because I'd really had no information at all – I didn't know how much I weighed, the hospital I was born in, what my name was, and that was quite enough to deal with at the time. It made it very much more real, yet it was also not real because it was like reading about somebody else. So it was a strange mixture of feelings really. I stored it away in the recesses of my mind and didn't really think about it much for quite a while. I was then 24 or 25 when I traced. I think I was getting older and it became important – I really don't know why, it just became important.❞

Apart from getting a clearer or fuller picture of a person's background and birth families, the other main reason for embarking on the search is the desire to establish some form of relationship with a birth relative. This might be prompted by what is found in the adoption record or it might be already established and the adoption record is merely a means to an end. As Ann commented, 'I always knew that I wanted to go right all the way to meet her'.

There are also several reasons why people decide *not* to search. Meeting a birth relative can be a daunting business and, as we shall see in later chapters, is very likely to have a major impact on the adopted person, the birth relatives and adoptive parents. The main reasons given for not searching by most of the 'information only' people in the research were based on a perception that it was the best way to protect the people involved, perhaps to protect themselves from rejection or a potentially difficult relationship, a desire not to disrupt the lives of the birth parents or not to hurt the adoptive parents. As Sandra commented:

> ❝I just had these thoughts of this nice cosy family and this letter coming through the door and maybe [my birth mother's] husband opening it. It's a shame, it would be

lovely if there was a way of doing it or finding out without actually making contact. I suppose if it was the other way as well, would she want to have too much contact with me and get to a situation where you know, I might upset my [adoptive] mother? So I don't know. Or it could work the other way, where you wanted more contact and she didn't. But the main reason was disrupting her life. And I'm working full-time and looking after my children. Life's just so busy anyway – you don't have a lot of time. I don't know, there might be a time a bit later on when things aren't quite so hectic, I'd got more time to do it. I'll make my mind up one day. I'm not good at making decisions. **"**

Of course none, or all, of Sandra's worries need be realised. Without searching she will not know how she or others might react or how things might turn out. What is important, however, is that she feels under no pressure to start a search. If, in the future, the time feels right for her, then searching remains an option.

How to go about your search

If you do decide to go ahead with the search, where do you start? What needs to be done? What sort of help is around? How should the first approach be made?

Fortunately over the last few years it has become much easier to search for birth relatives than previously. The task of locating birth relatives is not as onerous as it may have seemed when the adoption legislation first opened up the records over 25 years ago. There is much more knowledge available about how to search as well as more tools for locating information. There are now guides to searching, and modern technology such as the Internet has given people many more possibilities for locating birth relatives. There are self-help groups such as NORCAP (National Organisation for Counselling Adoptees and Parents) and many adoption agencies and local authorities will offer what advice and assistance they can to help you to find the birth relatives you may be searching for. But for adopted people who are just about to start on the journey of looking for and finding a birth relative, where do you begin?

In this chapter we take you through a step-by-step guide to how you can go about your search and the sorts of things you need to be aware of on your continuing journey. We have already described in Chapter 2 the first three steps you would need to take to obtain the information from your original birth certificate and access information that is held on the adoption record. Now we describe what to do next if you want to embark on a search for birth relatives. Although there are nine possible steps that you could take during the tracing stage, you may well find that you can locate a current address by just taking steps 2 and 3.

ADVICE BOX! ADVICE BOX! ADVICE BOX! ADVICE BOX! ADVICE BOX!

Outline of the stages and steps in searching and reunion

Tracing

1. Making the decision to trace birth relatives.

2. Current addresses: the electoral roll.

3. Current addresses: telephone directories.

4. Marriage certificates.

5. Birth certificates.

6. Divorce registers.

7. Death certificates.

8. Other directories.

9. Electronic sources and the Internet.

Making contact

10. Making the decision to get in contact with a birth relative.

11. Making contact (see below and also Chapters 4, 5 and 6).

Electoral roll

Once you have obtained information such as the names and addresses of other relatives from the adoption records you will need to check whether or not the relatives are still living at the addresses given at the time of the adoption. One way of doing this is to check the current electoral roll to find out if the person is still living at the stated address. Sometimes it is worth telephoning or writing to the local library or council electoral registration office for the area of the address to see if they can give you the information you need, or, if you have access to the Internet, a search for 'electoral roll' will lead you to sites offering to do a search for a fee. Since the Data Protection Act came into force some libraries and electoral registration offices will not divulge the information unless it is in writing, and they may also charge. However, the electoral rolls are public documents and, as a last resort, you could either go to the area yourself or find a friend who can look up the registers. Copies of the electoral records for all of England and Wales are kept at the British Library. However, if you want to look up past electoral registers, several days' notice is required. Further details about the procedure can be obtained by contacting the Official Publication and Social Science Section of the British Library (see Appendix).

Since the Data Protection Act people can choose not to have their details on these registers. This can be quite an attractive option as it cuts down 'junk mail' and 'cold calling' where companies try to sell you things. The electoral records are updated each year but those available to the public will not be comprehensive.

Telephone directories

The current address of the person you are looking for may be found in a telephone directory or by contacting directory enquiries (by phone or online). The telephone directories for England and Wales will be available at your local reference library. However, remember that not everyone is on a landline telephone, and as many people with landline telephones are ex-directory, this need not be your only route of enquiry – there are many other avenues.

If it appears that the relative you are looking for is living at the address you have obtained, then it is important to stop and think about how an approach should be made and who should do it. Normally, we recommend that you do not make a direct approach but use an intermediary. We will explain more about this later.

Checking the public records

If a current address cannot be found for the birth parent through the electoral roll or telephone directories, then a way forward is to check the public records for births, marriages and deaths. All birth, marriage and death records, as well as divorce records and wills, are public information and it is very often possible to trace people by this route. The information is held centrally for the whole of England and Wales at the Family Records Centre in London. Microfilm records of the birth, marriage and death registers can also be found at many local reference libraries, and the Office for National Statistics has a list of where these microfilm records can be found (see Appendix). The index to births, marriages and deaths for England and Wales can now also be searched online (see below under 'Electronic sources and the Internet').

Marriage registers

When trying to find a registration of marriage for either birth parent you should begin looking from the year that the birth parent was last known to be single. Marriage indexes list all the marriages alphabetically by name and in the quarter and year in which the marriage took place. If a marriage entry seems to be the one you are looking for, you can apply for a copy of the marriage certificate. This is a straightforward process that can be done through the post, or now online (see Appendix).

The certificate will give details such as age, occupation and the names of the couple being married. The marriage certificate also gives the address(es) of the couple at the time of their marriage. If the marriage certificate is found to be the correct one, then it is important to check the electoral roll again to find out if the address on the certificate is a current one. If it is not then you may still find out other information such as who was also living there at the time of the marriage and whether these other residents are still there. It is also worth rechecking the current telephone directory to see if a listing matches the initials and names on the marriage certificate.

Birth registers

If a marriage has been found, it is then possible to search the registers of birth. This helps to identify whether any children have been born of the marriage. Births are registered in the last name of the child, usually the father's name. The next column in the register states the birth mother's maiden name, which makes it easy to check if the child's parents are the people being looked for. However, there may be several possible entries and as all certificates applied for cost money, it is important to keep a note of all likely entries so that a decision on the most promising can be checked against the other information obtained via the adoption agency records.

If children of the marriage are registered and, at the time of searching, are 16 years and above, it is a good idea to check the index for a possible marriage entry. It may be that they married from the parental home, providing a more up to date address for the birth parent.

Divorce registers

You may also want to find out if the marriage ended in divorce, but this is a more costly process and probably should be done when all other avenues have been fully explored. Divorce registers are held at the Principal Registry of the Family Division in London (see Appendix). You are not allowed to search these registries yourself, but if you pay a fee of £20.00 a search covering a 10-year period will be done for you.

You could then go back to the marriage registers to see if the person you are looking for has remarried. Remember that when some women divorce they revert to their maiden name, so make sure you look up a marriage registration for all the surnames you have obtained.

Death registers

Another way to locate an up-to-date address is to look up a death registration for the paternal and maternal grandparents. You will obviously need to know the names of the grandparents and their dates or years of birth, which may have been included in the adoption agency record. If a registration is found then it is useful to obtain the death certificate as it will have the name and address of the person who registered the death, and this is quite often a relative.

If you have been unable to find details of a birth parent through the earlier steps, you might examine the death records in case they have died.

You can also see if the deceased person left a will. You can purchase a copy of the will or view it for a small fee. Although not everyone leaves a will, it can be a useful tool in the search process as the will contains the names and addresses of all the beneficiaries. This means that you may be able to find the birth relative you are looking for, or if not, perhaps another birth family member who could provide the other leads you need. You can get copies of wills by contacting the Probate Registry (see Appendix).

Other directories

Although most people can be found using public records, it is sometimes not possible to find an entry of any kind for the person being sought. In some situations where the person being looked for has a professional occupation, finding the person through the profession's directory could be another option. For example, *The Medical Directory*, *Institute of Chartered Accountants*, *Armed Forces' List* (Army, Navy and Air Force) can all be used. These directories can be found at most reference libraries. You could also look up *Kelly's Directory* in your local reference library as it gives information about well-known people.

Electronic sources and the Internet

In recent years, other resources to help people find family and friends have emerged. The one that most people are aware of is 'Friends Reunited'. This has been hugely successful, so using the Internet is certainly one way of exploring potential leads to help you to find the person you are looking for. You might also find information on birth relatives via search engines such as Google or Altavista.

Another useful resource is the InfoDisk. This CD contains thousands of names and addresses of people throughout England and Wales. All you have to do is, for example, put in the surname you are looking, let's say Joe Bloggs, and it will give you the names and addresses as well as phone numbers of every Joe Bloggs in the country. Or you can search for all 'Joe Bloggs' in Kent. Now that voters have the option to have their names left off the electoral register, the InfoDisk will have more gaps but it is still a very useful tool. The Family Record Centre in London has a copy of the InfoDisk but you can also purchase your own copy.

It is now also possible to do an online search of the registers of births, marriages and deaths for England and Wales via the Family Research Link website (see Appendix). The site does not provide the actual certificate but it will enable you to find the correct General Register Office reference number, which makes ordering the certificate easier and cheaper. There is a modest 'pay-per-page-view' charge. The site may be a useful resource particularly for people who cannot get to the Family Record office or reference library.

What if I cannot find any details?

Sometimes searches can be very difficult and frustrating. You discover that you always seem to reach a dead end. When this happens it is important to step back and think about why this might be, and decide the best way forward. For example, it could be that the birth relative you are looking for has moved abroad. If this is the case, then it is essential you seek the advice you need to help to locate someone in another country. It can be useful to contact NORCAP or perhaps the adoption counsellor who shared the adoption information with you, as they may have some useful tips and information about other avenues you could try. The Embassy for the country concerned will usually have a telephone directory that you can access. Libraries too may also hold telephone directories for other countries. St Martin in the Field's library in London, for instance, has the telephone directories for the United States on CD. This method can probably give you the specific details you need – for example, all those with the name O'Brien living in Detroit.

When things become difficult and you no longer feel able to search alone, you could seek the support of agencies like NORCAP or the adoption counsellor. Some people prefer to use a tracing agency, or private individuals who can undertake the search on their behalf. If you use this method, make sure you find out what it will cost, as this can be very expensive.

Life on the search trail

People's actual experience of searching will vary. In our study, some people found the search dull, tedious and sometimes frustrating; other people were clearly natural-born detectives enjoying the process of tracking down information. Part of the different reactions depended on how straightforward they found the search. Some searches were quick and simple – the record in our research was a few hours. Other searches took years, some having to be abandoning without success. Overall, however, 41 per cent of searchers found their birth mother's current address within a month, and 33 per cent found their birth father within the same time.

Yasmin was one of those who had a long frustrating search:

❝I did have somebody that I could just turn around and say 'look I really feel like shit' or 'I don't think I'm ever going to find her' or just somebody there. It took about two years. It felt like ages, I know some people search for like 10, 15 years – but I'm one of those people if I'm looking for it I want to find it now – not a year, two years. I knew it was going to take a long time – so I knew I had to be a bit more patient but it did feel like it took a long time. ❞

Although the search stage is probably the most practical bit of the whole searching and reunion process, it may not be just a technical exercise. After all, it is a search with a real purpose, of making contact with a birth relative. Some people feel very excited about the search as well as being very apprehensive about what might result; other people are keen to press ahead with the search but also feel guilty and disloyal because they may not have told their adoptive parents (we say more about this issue in Chapter 7). Even those who are the most detective-like in their approach can find themselves beginning to feel the emotional impact of the search, as Fraser reveals:

"Well every scrap of information you'd got was a stage further to your next step. I read it and read it and read it over and over again. And from that I built up a picture of things that I needed to do, in date time, where perhaps to go for that. One was searching electoral rolls for areas people had lived in at that time. It's a bit like a private detective and you're gaining information, planning that information so that you can make your next move, more successful possibly, than just blindly going and careering around and getting nowhere. Once you've got a successful piece of information I go and get that little bit of documentation and then I'd read that and move on. As you get more collected information you have, naturally, to get more involved. The more involved you get the more you personally, emotionally, will be affected and I think it's true to say that the clinical research was always in my mind but I was beginning to get embroiled in personal wishes by then. I think that happened within a year or maybe a fraction less of doing the research, I was now becoming embroiled in it. Once you get this information before you, whatever your plans were before, tend to go out the window."

Getting support during the search

The tracing stage can be just as much a 'rollercoaster experience' as other stages in the search and reunion process. This is certainly true for most people and you may also experience the highs and lows of a range of emotions and feelings as each new event unfolds. For this reason it is important that you have the support you need to help you along your journey. Support can come in a variety of ways, from someone accompanying you to the Family Record Office to having someone listen to your hopes and fears.

Many people find it helpful to join the self-help support groups that have developed around the world, e.g. NORCAP in England and Wales, Adopt in Northern Ireland or Birthlink in Scotland (see the Appendix for groups in other countries). These groups can be a great source of practical ideas, advice and energy as well as a means of emotional support and a sounding board. All the full contact details for these agencies can be found in the useful addresses given in the Appendix. Often, too, the adoption agency or local authority where you received either counselling and/or access to the adoption records are often willing and able to offer support, help and advice or, if not, put you in touch with someone who can.

Deciding whether or not to make contact

If you have managed to locate a current address for the birth mother or father or perhaps another birth relative, it is important not to rush forward, but to take stock before you make the next move. You have reached another decision point where you can go ahead and make contact, or pause for a while, or decide not to make contact for the foreseeable future.

There are a number of things you can do to help you to reach your decision or, if you have already made a decision to go ahead, to make sure you are as prepared as you can be. We recommend that you think through three questions, and write your answers down. The questions are:

- What are my expectations? Are they realistic? What if they are not met?
- What support will I have while making contact, both in the months and years afterward?
- Does it feel right for me to go ahead now?

It can be difficult to work your expectations out exactly. Quite often it is only when you meet a birth relative that it becomes clear what your expectations had been, either because you realise that you have found what you hoped for, or maybe because the reunion is not working out in some way. Even so, it is still vital to try to think through your hopes and expectations beforehand. It will help to talk them through with other people, such as friends and family as well as people with some experience of adoption, such as the adoption counsellor or a support group. If you can, talk to your adoptive parents (see more on this in Chapter 7). Do also read the rest of this book and gauge your emotional reaction to all the different stories – it may well give you some clues as to some of your 'secret' hopes as well as ideas for handling reunions. Write down your expectations before you set out, as the simple act of writing will really force you to explore your thoughts and feelings in much greater depth.

We have highlighted the importance of being as clear as you can about your expectations as they can really shape how the reunion begins and develops. Thinking through and perhaps adjusting your expectations may well help you to avoid entering the reunion with unrealistic hopes, as one of our interviewees, Ann, reported:

> **❝**My [adoptive] parents didn't want me to find her really, because they knew that I always had high expectations, I think they thought I was living in a fantasy world or something! I think they thought I was going to find her and just go and live wherever and have a wonderful life. But when the adoption counsellor gave me some books to read from the library I started to realise that it could be very different finding your birth mother, and that's when I came back and I thought this is actually something quite scary. And I felt really quite young as well, I was glad I had the counsellor as I couldn't do it on my own. I wanted to press ahead but I didn't want it to go wrong or anything and I didn't really know where I was heading at all really. But I'm definitely glad I've done it. And I was definitely glad that she recommended I read these books because otherwise I'd have expected it all to be over and done with in a couple of months and I wouldn't have known the implications.**❞**

Ann's account of her approach to contacting birth relatives emphasises the importance of having realistic expectations, but it also highlights the importance of having people to talk to about the process. Don't try to go through the reunion process on your own. It can help to talk with people beforehand, as well as for the months after, about the frustrations as well as the excitement.

Finally, when you have worked out your expectations and supports, the only remaining question is whether it feels right to go ahead now.

Making the approach

If you have a current address and have decided to make contact, the next decision is how to proceed. In a few cases a birth relative will have left a recent address with the adoption agency, perhaps inviting contact, but for most people the approach to the birth relative will be a step into the unknown. The adoption records may give some indication of how your birth mother or birth father felt about the adoption at the time. Your search through the records might have given you some further information about their current circumstances, such as whether or not they have married or have further children. But you are unlikely to know how either might respond to an approach *now*, whether they will be delighted, shocked, fearful or angry. Those initiating the search are likely to have been thinking about and preparing for a potential reunion for months or years. The person being contacted might have been thinking about you, or might have buried such memories long ago. In any case they are much less likely to be prepared for the approach at the particular moment that you decide to act. To protect both yourself and your birth relative, the approach needs to be conducted sensitively. There may well be a temptation to rush in, but it is critical at this point to think carefully and to try to handle the contact in a way that is least stressful for everyone involved.

There are three ways of making contact:

- **Adoption Contact Registers** – where adopted people and birth relatives independently express an interest in being put in contact with each other.
- **Intermediary approach** – where an adoption counsellor or other professional or friend makes the approach on behalf of the adopted person.
- **Direct approach** – where the adopted person approaches the birth relative in person.

We shall outline the pros and cons of each method below. Each has strengths and weaknesses but in most cases we caution against using a direct approach.

Adoption Contact Registers

Adoption Contact Registers have been set up in many countries by governments and adoption organisations over the last few years as a means by which adopted and birth relatives can make contact with each other where both parties seek it. Details about contact registers in the UK and Ireland, Australasia and North America can be found in the Appendix.

The Adoption Contact Register for England and Wales was set up by the government in 1991. The register is open to both adopted people and birth relatives. If both parties register, creating a 'match', then the General Register Office who run the register will inform the registered parties that there is a match and that they can make contact.

In theory the contact register should be a good way to make contact as it means that the adopted person and the birth relative have both signalled that they are interested in hearing from the other. In practice the register has not been publicised effectively and, consequently, few people know about it. By November 2000 only 18 276 adopted people and 8007 birth relatives had registered. Only 490 matches had been made since May 1991. Individuals may therefore register but a match might not be made, not because the birth relative does not want to be contacted but simply because he or she has not known about the register. Even so, we do recommend registering with the Adoption Contact Register, partly because the more people who are registered the better the service will perform, but, more importantly, if you are lucky enough to have a match you will be starting the reunion knowing that both parties want to have some contact. This can greatly reduce the amount of anxiety about a possible rejection.

One other disadvantage of the Adoption Contact Register is that the General Register Office does not offer counselling or support in thinking things through before or after a reunion. If you do go down the Adoption Contact Register route it is well worth talking things through – perhaps with the agency that handled your birth records information or a self-help organisation such as NORCAP – about how you might handle matters. Another disadvantage is that people do not have to confirm that they have received notification to say that there has been a match. Sometimes letters go astray in the post and the birth mother or the adopted person is left with the feeling that the other person no longer wants to make contact.

There is another contact register which is run by NORCAP, the self-help organisation for adopted people and their birth and adoptive relatives. Again, this is a useful tool although, as with the Adoption Contact Register, the fact that a birth relative has not registered does not necessarily mean that a contact would not be welcome. Details of NORCAP can be found in the Appendix.

As the contact register route is so little known, most people in England and Wales take either the intermediary or the direct approach.

Intermediary approach

Most adoption agencies or adoption support groups offer an intermediary service for adopted people (and increasingly for birth relatives also). The point of using an intermediary is that it provides an emotional buffer, giving birth relatives the opportunity to discuss their initial feelings and perhaps any concerns they may have as well as having support in deciding what response they wish to make. This is important because, irrespective of how an approach is made, it is likely to be a shock to the person being contacted without warning. Birth relatives are unlikely to be at the same point as you in terms of being ready for contact. While it may be something they have wanted for years, they may still need time to think through all the implications it has for them and their family. For instance, some birth mothers may be very keen to have contact with their son or daughter. However, they may not feel able to go forward with a meeting because they have not told their husband and children about the child they placed for adoption. For this reason a carefully worded letter from the intermediary will protect the birth mother's privacy but still have a clear meaning to her. A letter might, for example, be worded as follows:

> **❝**Dear——
>
> I am writing to you on behalf of John who you last saw in 1965 when you were living in London. He is well and settled but would like to make contact with you again. He has asked me to make this first approach to see how you would feel about this. I would appreciate it if you could telephone me so that I can give you more information.**❞**

If, say, the husband happens to open the letter, he would not immediately know from the letter that his wife had a baby placed for adoption. The birth mother can explain the letter in a way that is comfortable for her.

The intermediary could be someone who works in adoption as a counsellor, a volunteer, a partner, or a friend. Whoever is chosen must be someone whom you trust and who is comfortable with the intermediary role. Being an intermediary will usually involve much more than writing a letter. The intermediary will also need to handle any response from the person contacted. The response, as will become clear in later chapters, can range from wild excitement to anger or silence. If the response is not positive, finding a way through can be difficult, particularly if your choice of intermediary (say a friend or partner) has not had experience of adoption reunions. It might even be trickier if the intermediary has strong, protective loyalties to you. If at all possible, we recommend using an intermediary who is accustomed to making contact and has the experience, knowledge and skills often needed in these delicate and challenging situations.

The downside of using an intermediary can mean some delay in getting started. It also means that you are partly handing over the process to someone else. Usually, however, the delay is only a few days rather than months. As will be clear by now, we also think that getting support is helpful rather than unhelpful, although you will need to find an intermediary you can trust and in whom you have confidence.

Direct approach

Although the intermediary approach is the recommended route, we recognise that not everyone will want to use it. Some people, having obtained an address or a phone number, feel an overwhelming need to take action without delay, or feel that they want to be in control of the process. Making a direct approach can work, although it is potentially much more risky. One of our interviewees, Eleanor, wrote a letter directly to her birth mother, but in her case her birth mother, Diana, had already contacted the adoption agency to say that she would like to make contact. Eleanor had had access to the adoption agency's record and they had recorded Diana's wish for contact:

> **❝**I wrote a letter – 'blah, blah, blah, hope you didn't mind me writing . . .' talked a bit about who I was and what I did now, a bit about my childhood, I don't think I sent a

photograph with the initial letter. I wasn't sure if she'd reply – I was very scared that I'd upset her family, I was very anxious that I didn't . . . you know I was worried that someone else might open it and she hadn't told anyone and she'd be angry that I'd butted into her life. But her response was totally different. The next day I got home from work and there was a message on my answerphone – and it was my mother – I didn't expect her to ring – that was a bonus because I'd actually recorded it, I've still got it – it was really tearful – just saying 'it's Diana here, I've thought about you every day for 25 years', just so happy that I'd contacted her. And she said she was writing to me and I got a letter from her and some photographs and that was amazing. **"**

But the direct approach, particularly turning up at someone's door, can backfire. This form of approach can be seen as much more threatening and intrusive, giving the contacted person no chance to prepare or to take stock, and in some cases there may be an outright rejection. This was Debbie's experience:

"So once I'd got the address I went and phoned up. He [birth mother's husband] was extremely annoyed, extremely indignant – 'what right had I to phone his house, where did I get his address and phone number from?' and he obviously didn't realise that I was just around the corner. I made the fatal mistake of telling him where I was, went round and knocked on the door and of course they wouldn't open it, so I came back home, very very disillusioned, very very angry, even more angry then and I phoned her up the next day and I said 'look I'm sorry I know I blew it yesterday, but I was so wound up – having got an actual location for you' and she said to me as cool as anything 'I don't want anything to do with you, I gave you away 42 years ago and that is final, I don't want you to contact me again' and she put the phone down, and that was the last contact I've had with her and that was just a year ago. **"**

It is not possible to know for sure, but a more sensitive approach might have made a difference.

Summary

- We have set out a step-by-step approach for search and reunion. You may want to go through all the steps as quickly as you can, if that feels right, but take breaks or even long gaps if you need to.

- At each stage of the process make sure that you have support around you to talk through how things are going and what you might want to do next.

- If you decide to make contact, we recommend that you make use of any intermediary services that are available. Do not be tempted to go it alone unless you have clear indications that a direct approach would be welcome.

Reunions with birth mothers

For most adopted people, thoughts about birth parents during childhood were mainly about their birth mother. So most people begin their search hoping to make contact with her.

Introduction

We shall now look at what happens when contact is made. In this chapter we look at reunions with birth mothers, beginning with the first contact, on to the first meeting, and what happens thereafter. In the following two chapters, we first look at reunions with birth fathers and then consider contact with birth siblings. There is a very good reason for starting the reunion chapters with birth mothers rather than fathers or brothers or sisters. In practice this is what most reunions are about.

Our findings showed that 91 per cent of adopted people began their search by looking for their birth mother. It is also the case that birth mothers are most likely to search for adopted people. This is not a coincidence. Birth mothers often hold the information that adopted people want. They have some of the answers to questions such as 'who am I?' and 'why was I given up?' But more than this, it seems clear that there is a special emotional connection between birth mothers and their children.

The first contact

Making the first approach can be a delicate and anxious process, even if you use an intermediary, like the majority of people in our research. You might worry about being rebuffed or whether the approach might cause fear and distress. Clearly there can be no guarantees about what will happen in any individual case, but you may be encouraged and possibly surprised to hear that in our research the overwhelming majority of birth mothers agreed to have contact when first approached. Only 7 per cent of 274 birth mothers refused contact at this stage (see Chapter 8 for further details).

Although a very high proportion of birth mothers did agree to contact, how they actually felt about the prospect of reunion varied. Some birth mothers were clearly delighted at being approached. One of our interviewees reported that his birth mother's first words on the phone were 'I knew you would do it some day. I love you'. Another interviewee recalled a message on her answerphone in response to a letter saying that her birth mother had thought about her every day for 30 years and how thrilled she was to have been contacted. But not all birth mothers who agree to contact will be as enthusiastic. Some will be cautious and worried about what might happen, even if they do agree to go ahead. This was the case with Susan, whose birth mother was anxious about the prospect of reunion but was reassured by Susan's thoughtful letters:

> ❝The counsellor wrote to my birth mother and said she had met me and I would like to write to her and could I have permission. My birth mother wrote back and said 'yes but they were fairly old and they didn't want any problems' as such. And I wrote them a very long letter but it was very much a light-hearted letter, which couldn't possibly be threatening. Just saying who I am and what I'd done over the years and what sort of person I was and how I would like to know a bit about my history and I got a really nice letter back from them and then we met a few months later.❞

There are a number of ways to move forward after the initial contact. You can choose to start off by exchanging a series of letters, perhaps using the adoption counsellors as a neutral 'letterbox'. The advantage of this approach is that it gives you a chance to find a little bit more about each other before meeting, about the past and current circumstances, and something of each other's personality. It also provides an opportunity to exchange photographs. Where either the birth mother or the adopted person, or perhaps both, are nervous or apprehensive about the prospect of reunion, then letters can be a really good place to start, as in Jessica's reunion:

> ❝It got to the point where I was really looking forward to getting her letters and I think I realised just from the way she wrote that there was something there. I found it more and more easy to write to her. How can I explain? We just had a very similar style in the way that we wrote – quite sensitive and caring but also holding back on things because of not wanting to upset the other one. Then we sent each other photos – I sent her five or six photographs of me throughout my life. I said in the letters that 'I don't want to rush this, it is such a big thing for me that I just want to take it a step at a time and I hope you can understand this – if I rush into meeting you then it will be too much too soon'. Looking back on it, it was exactly the right thing to do really.❞

Although exchanging letters might be a good place to start for some people, it is not going to be right for everyone. Some people find writing letters impossible, and simply do not know where to begin or what to say. Equally, not everyone wants to take things slowly. When both sides are keen to move forward, you could have the first meeting very quickly. In our research Harry's first meeting was probably the shortest, taking just a few hours from reading the adoption record to making contact via an intermediary and then the first meeting:

> ❝My wife said 'there's a woman on the phone for you'. So I said 'hiya' and she said 'It's your mum here'. We were on the phone for about an hour talking about anything and everything, I wouldn't even like to hazard a guess at what we talked about. I then said to her 'well could I speak to my sister, what do you reckon?' She said 'yes, she knows about you, she's always known about you'. So I rang my sister up, who was by

then expecting me to phone. Then mum phoned back a bit later in the morning. I got absolutely nothing done. I was just on cloud nine. I then said to her 'well look, I seem to know you now, can we meet?' She said 'OK'. I said 'do you want me to come to you, or you come to me?' She said 'well you can come round to me if you like'. So we went round and saw her that evening. **"**

In Harry's case this rapid move to actually talking to his birth mother worked out well. As always, however, the way things turned out will be different for different people. Not everyone finds the first phone call easy or has the same level of shared excitement to carry the conversation along. For some people the first phone conversation is hesitant and difficult, with both sides struggling to know where to begin or what to say. Remember that the first conversation will not necessarily be an accurate guide to how the reunion will develop once you have met and had time to get to know each other, as Joanna notes:

"It was a bit stilted, a bit kind of 'like what do you say?' We didn't talk about how we felt or anything. There was lots of like 'god this is really weird' and 'this is so strange' type thing. She was very very quiet on the phone, it was a very difficult conversation. I found it extremely difficult to get anything out of her. Knowing her now, that is how she is on the phone. But at the time I was thinking 'she doesn't want to talk to me, why are there all these huge gaps?' **"**

ADVICE BOX! ADVICE BOX! ADVICE BOX! ADVICE BOX! ADVICE BOX!

The first contact

- Think carefully about the best way of making contact. Think about how you would want to be contacted if the situation were reversed.

- Keep an open mind if the first conversation is harder than you thought it might be. You are both in a strange situation. Wait to see how things develop before making a judgement.

- Take a deep breath after making the first contact. Do not let yourself be rushed into meeting straight away, or push the other person to meet you before she is ready. Letters, emails and phone calls can be a good way to get to know a bit about each other first. They also give you time to think about what is happening. But if you both feel that it is right to meet as soon as you can, then go ahead.

- Talk to as many people and get as much support as you can before, and after, you make the first contact. Another advantage of using an experienced intermediary is that he or she will be able to help you to be as prepared as possible before making contact and be a valuable sounding board for how you are feeling once contact is made.

The first face-to-face meeting

If the first phone conversation is an anxious affair, the first face-to-face meeting can an even more nervy experience however much you are wanting it to happen. Regardless of how much previous contact there has been, there is nothing quite like the first face-to-face meeting, as Patrick describes:

> **❝**The first meeting? I mean obviously it was a difficult day. It's difficult to describe how difficult it is. Suddenly sort of actually meeting someone that you've thought about for a long time is a nerve-wracking experience. And it's the same for her, I mean she was nervous. We got on very well, immediately, thank God! Difficult day though. I think it's probably different for everybody but it's something that you can't really put into words, do you know what I mean? It's not possible; words aren't really sort of enough to explain the feelings involved. It's a whole mixture of things, you know the apprehension, you know, happiness, sadness. The whole thing really, it's a real cock-tail and that's why it's probably difficult because life doesn't really prepare you for that sort of thing in a way, do you know what I mean? I mean I felt nervous, I definitely felt nervous! It's very difficult you know knocking on the door. I mean some people would say no there wasn't any difficulty, but it depends on who you think you are I think. We're all different.**❞**

Many people describe the first meeting as one of the most nerve-wracking experiences of their lives, mentioning pounding hearts, shaking hands and dry mouths as they walk up to a door or await someone's arrival. This level of worry and anxiety, even fear, is understandable for lots of reasons. For most people the first meeting is the point where you finally come face-to-face with the person you have thought and wondered about for years, often as the culmination of a long search. This is a meeting between a mother and child, one of the most significant relationships in any culture, but where each knows very little about the other. It is inevitable that the meeting is loaded with meaning and expectations. As you are wondering whether the other person matches up to your hopes and expectations, you will both be trying to work out what the other is feeling. No wonder many people find it hard to recall exactly what happened in the meeting or what they talked about.

Another highly charged issue for many adopted people is meeting for the first time someone you look like or are related to. Even if you do exchange photographs before the first meeting, that will not necessarily prepare you for the impact of coming face-to-face with a blood relative. Although not everyone sees physical similarities, many people in our research were struck by shared mannerisms and characteristics. Wendy's description of her first meeting with her birth mother captures some of the emotional turmoil and wonder of the situation:

> **❝**I saw her getting out of the car and I knew it was her because of the way she walked. When she walked in, she looked at me and she said 'how you've grown but you are exactly the same'. I just found myself looking at her a lot. I couldn't believe that I could

look like somebody else. I do remember looking – and I remember the voice – and the mannerisms, it was weird. I think so much gets taken in – and everything on the surface is very superfluous – the words don't really matter because you spend a lot of time looking at each other – sizing up, what's going on, what's been going on? I don't know that I thought she gave birth to me – she certainly didn't feel like 'mummy' but the bond was instant – it was there, especially when somebody looks so much like you – that's the thing I probably latched on to the most – 'I look like somebody' – it's very strange. I think you take everything inwardly, you're talking but you are not paying attention, you're watching what's going on, it's most peculiar. **"**

How connected you feel to each other and what that connection will feel like is not easy to predict. In our research, most people's reaction to the first meeting was positive, but the degree of 'connectedness' varied. Twenty-six per cent of people found the first reunion meeting an intense, emotional experience in which they felt an 'instant connection' to someone who felt like 'mum'. Harry, who we met above, had a very fast reunion with his birth mother and explains:

"She had one photograph of me in her arms in the mother and baby home. That's all they were allowed. The idea was to stop bonding. But I was so much like her. Without having met her at all, everything – mannerisms, the way I move my hands, the way I talk, every single thing. Except for the accent we are two peas out of a pod, there's no way she's not my mum. So they failed totally in stopping any bonding. Basic instincts. I just knew – that's mum. I'm part of her and that bond was just instantly there. **"**

There was a large proportion of people (46 per cent) who did feel positive after the first meeting but described the relationship as more like a 'friend' rather than an instant mother–child relationship. Kim, for example, was delighted to meet her birth mother but did not feel immediately that she was like a 'mother':

"We spent a day in London and that went very well, very well indeed. You know just sitting in a cafe, sort of looking at the shape of our hands and things like that. We don't look very much alike at all but we have a lot in common about the way we see things and the way we think about things. So it was a very good day, a very good day. I didn't feel that she was my mother. She was just some nice person I wanted to meet really. She's one of those people you look at and you think 'oh that's a nice lady' you know. **"**

It is important to point out that reunions that are initially described as 'friend-like' can work out just as well as those where there is an 'instant connection'. Starting out as friends can be a realistic approach to developing a strong and positive relationship over time, where you both work out the kind of relationship you want, given that you are both now adults.

We should also stress that not everyone looks for, or is comfortable with, an instant 'mother–child' connection. A more low-key approach is preferable for some people, as it was for Edward:

"I was very nervous waiting, and suddenly I saw this woman and I thought that's her. I patted her on the back and said hello. She said hello. It wasn't emotional at all. It was 'come on let's go and grab a pizza then'. It was very informal, very laid-back, just how I wanted it. We had a great chat, and I took her back to the station and we had a hug and a kiss when I said goodbye to her."

Although the majority of people feel positive about first meetings, a minority of people are less comfortable, even awkward. For 26 per cent of people, the reunion felt like meeting a stranger, feeling confused or distant. Lucy had one of those meetings in which there was no connection:

"Neither of us were emotional. We both chain smoked a lot and I think we had alcohol. I mean it's difficult to think, to remember what I felt like then and what I feel like now. But I think there was a slight bit of disappointment that she's just like this ordinary sort of working-class woman and she's not, you know, somebody special! Which I think I would have liked really. We got on as well as you'd meet somebody socially and you could manage to spend a couple of hours with them. There was no like antagonism between us but it wasn't like a big connection. I think we were both too scared for that really. So no, there wasn't a big connection, and has never been actually."

Gill's experience was similar, finding the first meeting very uncomfortable:

"I thought 'oh she's old' and I thought 'well she's got to be old, she's in her 60s what did you expect'. I suppose I'd always thought of her as still being 27. So that was a shock – she just said 'oh, hello, come in', no big hugs or kisses, she was very stand-offish. First impressions I didn't think she looked like me. She was just all big long pauses and I didn't really know what to say. Half the time I was thinking 'I wish I wasn't here' and then I kept staring at her trying to see similarities and yes she does look like I will probably look in a few years time. But the strange thing was my husband took a photo of us and we are both standing there with our hands with the middle finger and thumb clasped together and that was quite uncanny."

ADVICE BOX! ADVICE BOX! ADVICE BOX! ADVICE BOX! ADVICE BOX!

Where and how to meet

- There's no ideal venue that will suit everyone. A lot will depend on how well you've got to know each other and your initial reactions to each other.

- A neutral venue, such as a pub, restaurant, hotel or park might be a good choice as there will be other people meeting and greeting; ▶

however, it may feel too public for some people as it offers limited privacy.

- A good meeting place could be one or other's home as this will offer more privacy. However, some people might feel less comfortable on someone else's 'territory'. One alternative might be at the home of a third party. Occasionally people like to meet at the post-adoption service office and most agencies will make a room available.

- It is probably best to arrange to meet for just a few hours at first. You can always decide to extend it if it is going well. But do not forget that the first meeting is likely to be emotionally draining for both of you and you will need a break.

- If you live far apart, and one of you has to travel a long distance, it is usually best to arrange to stay in a hotel or B&B, even if you are invited to stay in someone's home. It might seem a bit stand-offish but both of you will need some space to gather your thoughts. There are, however, no hard and fast rules. If it feels right to stay at someone's home then do so, but not if you are feeling pressured.

- Sometimes it can help to have someone with you at the first meeting, either a partner, friend or counsellor. Sometimes a third party can help to ease what can be a difficult situation. Make sure, however, that the person will be able to handle the situation and work for you rather than feel excluded or jealous.

Coming down and moving on?

For most participants the first meeting raises complex emotions – some positive, some negative. Often people feel exhaustion or distress. Owen, who described a very positive first meeting, nonetheless also felt upset driving away. The feelings that are stirred can remind people of the lost years and, for some, there is the fear of losing the person again. For others, the dominant emotions are those of confusion, hurt or disappointment.

For all the anxiety and excitement and possible disappointment generated by the initial meeting, the reunion process for most people is far from being over. Having got over the first major emotional hurdle you then need to think about your next step. In some cases this issue is discussed at the first meeting, with clear plans to phone or meet again. In other cases, it is left open and the next task is to work out together what happens next. Or you might have already decided that you do not want to meet again, at least for a while. Whatever applies to you, it is important to pause and reflect on what has happened before moving forward. We cannot stress enough how draining the first meeting is for most people. For the majority, it is a real high, but can be followed almost immediately by a sinking feeling as the excitement, even euphoria, of the reunion fades away and the reality of daily life returns.

Not everyone has the same reaction, not least because the experience of the first meeting varies so much. It is nevertheless important to be as prepared as you can be *after* the first meeting as well as *before* it. If at all possible, try to re-establish some of your normal routines that might have fallen by the wayside over the course of the search. If you can, take a break, or at least give yourself time to think about and absorb all that has happened. Make sure that you get a chance to talk with people about how the meetings have gone and how you would like things to develop.

ADVICE BOX! ADVICE BOX! ADVICE BOX! ADVICE BOX! ADVICE BOX!

What to do if you don't feel any connection with or get on with your birth mother

- Don't despair, most people do not experience an instant bond (or do not want to). It does not mean that the reunion is doomed.

- Acknowledge how you are feeling – are you disappointed or are you, perhaps, relieved?

- Think about your hopes and expectations for the reunion. Not everyone is looking for an instant connection or a 'mother–child' relationship.

- Think about why you might be feeling like this. The first meeting is a very unusual and emotionally charged situation with neither of you behaving as you would 'normally'. What were your expectations? How might you feel if you were meeting that person simply as a new potential friend or work colleague? Try to work out what the reunion means to you both. Either of you might be experiencing feelings of rejection, loss or guilt. Or you, or your birth mother, might be just shy or reserved with everyone.

- Don't forget that you cannot choose your relatives. Biological links are very important but they don't mean that you will automatically share the same values, traits or interests. You are likely to have different lifestyles because of your different histories as well as belonging to different generations. Mother–child relationships, ▶

where there has been no separation, have had decades to grow and develop, and can still be very fraught! Take time to get to know each other and be prepared that it may take several years to work out a comfortable way of relating.

- Talk to other people that you trust such as a counsellor, partner or support group, and ask them to help you to think about how the other person might have felt or be feeling about the reunion.

- Communicate with the other person, by letter if that is easier. If you found the meeting really difficult, then say so. You might find that the other person is relieved and will be able to be honest with you, giving you a foundation for moving forward.

- The other person might simply be very difficult and prove to be someone that you could never get on with or find a place for in your life. If so, let that person, and yourself, down gently.

Reunions over time

Most outsiders would probably think of an adoption reunion as that first meeting, but in practice most reunions need to be seen as a long-term process, not a one-off event. We have seen how differently people react to the first meeting. Now we turn to look at what happens next with birth mother reunions. How do they develop over time? Do they last? What kinds of relationships are established? Can reunions with a rocky start get established and if there is a good start how might that bode for the future?

Most reunions do have a stickability factor. In our research 76 per cent of people were still in contact with their birth mother three years after their first meeting; and even eight years or more later, 55 per cent were still in touch.

The most *typical* pattern that reunions take over the long term is to go through a honeymoon period, followed by a cooling down before a gradual settling down into a long-term, sustainable pattern with all the normal ups and downs. The honeymoon phase is usually the most intense period, with frequent contact between the pairing. In many cases, this can quickly take in a whole network of other birth relatives and friends. This is the period of starting to get to know each other, and is tinged with the initial excitement and wonder of the first meeting. Many people tend to see a lot of each other in the first year, speaking and writing frequently. Twenty-five per cent of people who had actively sought their birth mother were having face-to-face contact with her at least once a month. If we just look at telephone calls and letter writing, then 6 out of 10 people were in touch at least once a month during their first year of reunion.

The level of contact and intensity of the relationship gradually scales back as time passes, sometimes with one party 'cooling off' a little, or where both reach a point when they do not need such frequent contact to sustain the relationship. Eventually most settle down and the 'new' relationship becomes part of everyday life. In our study, for example, five years after first meeting, almost 70 per cent of those who had searched for their birth mother were still in some kind of contact, albeit on a less intense basis. Typically, in about a quarter of those still in touch, face-to-face contact was taking place at least once every three or four months, supplemented in many cases with telephone calls. It is worth pointing out that there is very little difference in the average frequency of contact between those adopted people who searched for their birth mother and the non-searchers whose birth mothers contacted them through an intermediary. It seems that once the relationship is established, who initiated it, whether the adopted person or the birth mother, ceases to be of great importance.

So far we have been careful to talk about what happens in the 'average' reunion to give an idea of how many last and at what level of contact. But behind the averages there are great differences in how reunions with birth mothers evolve. Some reunions never get to the honeymoon stage. Some just tail off by mutual agreement after each person feels that all questions have been answered or that maintaining contact is on balance just too complex (we look at reunions that break down after a single meeting in Chapter 8). Although reunions can last for years, with many being relatively straightforward, others can be much more tricky to manage. To really get at the real nature of reunions and how relationships develop we need to listen in more depth to the stories of our interviewees.

Different styles and states of relating

We have seen how initial reactions to the first meeting vary. This is just as true for reunions over the long term. Inevitably, given that there are two people coming together for the first time, working out the relationship can be difficult for some. Examining the reunion stories we found that there were five different styles of relating:

- **Balancing:** both members of the pairing have the same expectations of the reunion, place broadly similar importance on the relationship and the relationship feels easy and comfortable.
- **Distancing:** one member of the pairing feels that the other is too intense or pushy and so attempts to hold the other at bay.
- **Testing:** one, or possibly both, members of the pairing feel that the other person is not committed enough to the reunion and attempts to make the other person demonstrate some commitment.
- **Drifting:** the reunion is never really established and the pairing gradually ceases contact.
- **Overloading:** one of the pairing places too many demands with which the other is unable to cope, sometimes resulting in a rejection.

In the remainder of the chapter we explore these ways of relating in much more detail. However, we should point out that these styles are not necessarily always fixed or set in stone. In many cases they are more 'states' or 'stages' which people go through in the relationship, possibly ending up in the 'balanced' state. To illustrate how dynamic and changeable the relationship can be, we end this chapter by looking in a little more detail at three reunions that have followed very different patterns.

Balancing

Some pairings manage to find a comfort zone at an early stage, where both are committed to the reunion at similar levels of intensity, with no real problems in working out their relationship. Everything seems comfortable from the start. Other pairs, as we see below, go through all kinds of different and difficult phases before reaching a balance. However, it is really important to point out that there is no blueprint for reaching this comfort zone. Different pairings reach a balance at very different levels of closeness. For some the balance means a mutually intense and vital relationship. Other pairings find a balance at a lower, sometimes much lower, level of intensity, but it is still what each member seems to want.

High-pitch balance

For some reunion participants the early part of the reunion is indeed a honeymoon period, with adopted people and their birth mothers needing a lot of contact in the early months. There is a lot of getting to know each other, trying to fill in the decades of separation over a few months. Over time the level of contact gradually scales down but with a strong sense from both partners that this is likely to be a lasting and important relationship. Olive and Owen both illustrate this high-pitched but balanced state:

> ❝For the first year we had to have absolute regular contact, physical contact, we had to see each other once a month for the first year. That's how it was, there was a definite need for both of us to maintain this contact. That's what we did that first year until things settled down. I had a sense of loss because I hadn't had her for so many years, a loss because of my own [adoptive] mum [who had died], but complete happiness because we were together and it had gone so well and it was more perfect. We were totally connected. And we still are after almost 10 years. It's just settled into a normal family relationship. So normal it's unbelievable, they are my family. My second family. I was totally accepted by the whole family.❞
>
> Olive

> ❝I was very comfortable in her house – and it felt like home anyway – which makes her very happy, it still does, to this day. I feel very comfortable there. From then on we've gone from strength to strength. After about five months I suppose it started to come down a bit – we got used to the idea – we'd gone through the initial stages of going to The Children's Society, letters, phone calls, meeting, then meeting all the family. I suppose it was an impossible level to maintain anyway and gradually we came

back down to earth – we got used to the idea. We still phone twice a week and I go up once a month – and I thought perhaps after a year or so it might wane but it hasn't. It will one day I suppose but when, we don't know, that will come naturally when we both feel we can move away a little bit. **"**

Owen

Low-pitch balance

It is also possible to move forward together but at a much slower pace and in a much more low-key fashion. If this is what both the adopted person and birth mother want, then this can be an equally successful reunion as the high-pitch balance. Colin's reunion was much less intense than those of Olive or Owen, but both he and his birth mother seemed comfortable with the relationship they had established:

"It has been well matched. We tend to speak on an irregular basis, we speak every three months or so – it's not hard and fast – just pleasantries 'how are you, what have you been doing since we last spoke'. The last three years I've seen my natural mother about once a year. I do keep in touch. Perhaps not on a regular basis but then I don't talk to many people on a regular basis – other than my immediate friends and colleagues and the like. It's comfortable yes. I've not felt pressurised to make contact more so than I do, and it's not been suggested that they see me too often either. I don't know if they would like to see me more, but certainly the invitation's there if I feel inclined to do so. I don't think they'd push it. I probably still treat it like it now, like having an extended family of aunts and uncles. There is a bit of a difference I suppose, the natural mother is slightly more than just another aunt. **"**

The state of balance, whether at high or low pitch, or somewhere in between, seems to be the easiest and most relaxed phase of reunion, and probably what most people hope to achieve. Some people are lucky enough to fall into this pattern from the beginning, others have to work through more difficult patches or stages to get there. The key task for those who are in the 'balanced' state, particularly those who begin at a high pitch, is to ensure that you do not fall into the trap of idealising the other person. This means acknowledging the other person's weaknesses as well as strengths, and feeling able to argue and disagree, tackling some possibly difficult questions about the circumstances of the adoption. In the early stages the relationship can seem too fragile to handle different views and opinions, particularly as you have only just reunited. But to develop a realistic relationship you need at some point to address these issues, but only when you feel ready.

Pam, one of our interviewees, recognised that her relationship with her birth mother was still at the rose-tinted stage where both were still protecting each other. At some point they would feel secure enough in the relationship not to have to agree about everything:

"We haven't had an argument or anything yet – which suggests that perhaps we are still going through a honeymoon period – I don't know. Because any mother–daughter relationship – normal mother–daughter relationships – you fall out over things don't you – well I do with my adoptive mother so . . . I haven't had to handle that yet. I'm sometimes conscious of things that I say to not upset her. So there's a certain fragility there. And yet it's nothing like as fragile as it was – I think it's just going to be a gradual process. I'm just a very cautious person anyway and I think she is. **"**

Distancing

The critical thing about the 'balanced' way of doing reunions is that the expectations and commitment to the reunion of the different participants are similar, whether at high, mid or low pitch. Where one side has different expectations and a different commitment, then making the reunion work can be more difficult. For some pairings the reunion goes through a phase or stays at a level where one person wants a slower or less intense reunion and is concerned about being 'swamped' or taken over by the other person. It can be either the adopted person or birth mother who holds the other at bay. This situation needs careful handling to avoid being pushed further and faster than either person wants, while recognising that slowing it down might hurt the other's feelings. This is not an easy task, particularly given the lack of experience that both have in working out differences together.

The adopted person slows things down

David is a good example of 'the take it slow' approach in the early stages of a reunion where the birth mother's expectations and need for contact were greater than his. His account highlights the need he had to stay in control of the situation while his birth mother wanted to go much faster and to take on the 'mother' role. But it also reveals the unease, even guilt, of not being able to match the other person's expectations of the relationship:

"It was two months between ringing her and meeting her. I mean she wanted me to get a flight the next day. I also made the decision 'no I'm not going to do that'. It all happened so quickly and I thought I would do it in my own time and I'll do it when I'm ready. She can't expect me to just go running over there and drop everything else that has happened in my life. I made a conscious decision she was not going to come into my life and not possibly disrupt anything. I went alone. I stayed in a hotel. . . . I suppose the phases went something like – elation, when I met her and having solved a few questions in my head – to her being very possessive – to me not knowing, wanting to know her anymore – to, no in-between that, she, it was like having another woman in my life, not necessarily my mother – and then for me, not wanting to bother any more – to settling down to probably just contacting her about once a month or something like that. But saying that, I haven't contacted her for about three months now. I don't know she seems to talk about herself all the time and I'm not the sort of person that will talk about myself all the time – I'm more interested in other people, but saying that it's all 'her, her, her', or it was for a stage. We went through a phase that she thought, I think,

I was a little boy and she wanted to be a mother. So it was quite cruel at the time, a lot of people didn't understand that, that I was stand-offish. **"**

Birth mothers slowing things down/holding back

Some birth mothers are also very cautious in their approach to the reunion, which moves forward more slowly than the adopted person might wish. Again this difference in expectations requires delicate handling to enable the reunion to move forward. Susan was able to use her professional training to keep her reunion alive, but also had to accept that the reunion was less intense than she might have wished:

> **"**I think my professional training helped me a lot because I treated it very much like a younger person meeting an older person and I tried to build up trust, friendship and not being too over-emotional about it all. We haven't had a really serious, in-depth conversation. They've made me feel very welcome but I also know that she doesn't want me to get too involved so the fact that I perhaps see her once or twice a year is the way she wants it. She just doesn't want the rest of her family to know about me and I think she's a bit worried that that's going to happen. It's coming up to about five to six years. I feel as though I have got as far as I can go and I also accept the fact that it's still very much treading on fairly shaky ground and it has to be done carefully. So I think it's fairly much how we both want it in that we are not intruding on each other's lives too much, although I would have liked to have had a little bit more. I think that's perhaps because she's just getting literally too old to want to do it. And I certainly don't want to pressurise her in any sort of way. **"**

It is not surprising that some reunions are imbalanced in terms of commitment and intensity. Unlike a friendship that is built up over time, but may be abandoned early on if there is imbalance, in a reunion, both sides find themselves suddenly thrown into the relationship. It is a fact of life that some people are very outgoing and emotional while others are more reserved. Inevitably, reunions throw together different personalities. We also need to take account of adoption-related factors which can make a difference. This can be just about different generations meeting. Or it might be fear of the strong claims and strong emotions that suddenly erupt as the reunion becomes real. Reunion participants can then want to protect themselves or the rest of their families from a possibly overwhelming new relationship.

In Susan's case, it was her birth mother's worry about other family members finding out about the adoption; for others it might be a sense of loyalty to the adoptive family that makes people hold back. There can be other in-built factors too. Birth mothers who have not had further children might want a more 'parent–child' relationship to develop than the 'child' feels comfortable with.

So there are many reasons why there might be an imbalance in the relationship. When this occurs, most people are able to deal with it over time, although there can be uncomfortable moments. Part of the trick is to accept that it is likely that differences will occur, and that in all types of relationships people often place different priorities on things but they can still be managed. If you are the person who is being kept at a distance then it might be worth thinking through your expectations. You might try to adjust to your birth mother's pace at an early stage and see how things develop. If you are the one feeling under pressure to give more, then it might help if you try to explain to her that you do want the relationship to develop but that you need to pace it more. These can be difficult conversations. It means that you are giving clear messages that you are not going to disappear, but you need a little more space. Over time you may both find a comfortable balance even though you place different emphases on the reunion.

Testing

Another pattern, and one that seems difficult to break, is that of 'commitment testing'. Here the adopted person or birth mother wants the other person to commit to the relationship but is very unsure of his or her commitment. The result is a push–pull pattern of wanting more commitment from the other but being unable to express this need, leaving one or other of you feeling frustrated or let down. Occasionally people threaten to withdraw or goad the other into expressing their love.

There are lots of reasons why people might not click. Different personalities or different lifestyles might act as a barrier to a relationship's development. But the emotional issues specific to adoption and reunion can be difficult to manage without outside help. Although many people have an understandable fear of rejection and so play their cards close to their chest, adopted people might feel particularly vulnerable. Lucy's reunion with her birth mother illustrates some of these issues. Their reunion was difficult, characterised by ambivalence where both seemed too anxious to express their feelings, or to allow each other fully into their lives. Lucy wanted her birth mother to demonstrate her love for her but found it hard to express that wish openly until her mother had given her a clear message that she did love her. In this type of push–pull situation both parties are probably getting mixed messages about what the other wants and may interpret this as a lack of care and interest. As a result, both may feel let down:

> "There was a time when we actually got quite close – she went away on holiday and she brought me back a present and I remember being extremely touched by it and I like it when she acts like a mum. I want her to do more of the running. I want it to be more like a mother and child relationship whereas I can be offhand with her and she makes the running really. It's terribly juvenile really isn't it! But that's how I feel. For instance it was my thirtieth birthday and she sent me a card, this poxy card. I know this sounds very sort of petulant and demanding, but I would like her to just do more. I'd like to feel more cosseted by her. I'd like to feel more loved by her. But I don't feel that I have to respond! I'd just like to feel more loved by her. I don't want to feel more loving. Yeah, I'd have to get it first! So my feeling loving towards her feels quite conditional on me receiving something from her first. I have a feeling of wanting her to kind of make it up to me. I want to get more from her, but I feel reluctant to put more into it. I feel like it's her job, I feel like she's the grown up, I'm the child, it's her job. She's the one that has to make it up to me so she should do the running. But its now

a bit distant. Not very real. I think a bit superficial, a lot of unexpressed things. Not close. But I mean I'm glad, I'm very glad I met her but it's not like one of the kind of deeper relationships of my life. It's more like an obligation. **"**

Ava's reunion with her birth mother was also ambivalent. The issue of rejection also seemed to play a part. In Ava's case, as with others, it was hard for her to feel she was liked for herself, rather than just because she happened to be her birth mother's daughter. Some people in this situation can feel that they are not entitled to the relationship. As a result people, like Ava, who are uncertain about their right to the relationship, offer to withdraw, almost getting their rejection in first. The uncertainty about the relationship can also mean keeping the other person at a distance while at the same time trying to provoke someone into making a response:

"I said 'if you don't want this to continue you only have to say' – because as far as I'm concerned I just class them as friends. My adoptive mum and dad, they are mine. There was a time when I was finding myself being quite abrupt with her – when we were round there I was trying to get a response out of her almost, I was baiting her. I do feel that some of my mannerisms with her are a bit unnatural. They are not me. I don't really feel I can be 100 per cent natural with her. I think I would be a little bit upset or put out if she decided to break with me, but I would understand. And I can't quite understand why she would want to know me actually. She doesn't have to like me just because I'm her natural daughter and it shouldn't be an unconditional thing. I was on the phone to her trying to get across to her 'just because I'm your birth daughter it doesn't mean you have to carry on with this' because I had noticed that she's quite quiet and it's a bit of an effort to keep the conversation going. She was getting really upset about it, she was getting quite tearful, so she obviously does think quite a lot of me and she doesn't want me to just break the relationship. **"**

It can be hard to break out of a cycle where neither side is saying how they really feel or clearly stating what they want from the relationship. Each may feel that the other does not really care or care enough. This is not just a reunion problem; this happens in many relationships. There are strategies you can use to try to move things on. The first is to take another look at your expectations. Are they realistic and reasonable? It may help to talk to someone outside of the situation such as a friend or a counsellor. The second strategy is to communicate how you really feel and how you would like the relationship to be rather than use indirect ways of trying to get what you want. If it is too difficult to do this face-to-face, then it might be easier to write a letter.

Drifting

For some pairs, the reunion never gets properly established and contact gradually dwindles to virtually nothing. This is not due to any major problem or disagreement but simply that those involved never really click or establish a connection they both want to continue. Here is Adrian's account of his reunion:

"When I met her it was all very strange because she didn't look like me at all. So that was a bit of a let-down I suppose. I saw her a few times a year but I don't really connect with her in a big way really. I don't want a mother in my life but a friend would be nice, but trying to forge a friendship with somebody who's 30 years older than you and you've not got a lot in common with, it's quite difficult to do really. Fundamentally, what time I had I wanted to give it to my [adoptive] mother cause she needed it. And the thing about it was about my cultural identity. There might have been more motivation to keep it going but they were very, very English and there was no motivation, nothing there to help me develop my cultural identity by forging a relationship with these people. But I tried to be as civil as possible. A lot of my motivation is still for selfish reasons really, to try and find out a bit more about me. I don't know which way it's going to go but quite possibly it's fizzling out, but I'd like to keep in touch in some way if I can, even if it's just a once a year scenario."

Adrian's story highlights that a simple biological connection does not necessarily mean that you will find anything in common with your birth mother. You are, in effect, strangers from different generations often with quite different backgrounds. In many cases an emotional tie does develop but, as we have seen, it does not happen in every case. The lack of a connection might just be one of those things. Or it may relate to your hopes and expectations. Not everyone is seeking to establish a significant relationship. Some people set out with a much stronger focus on finding information about their roots and the circumstances of their adoption – information that they can only find from their birth mother. A relationship with a birth relative might be a bonus but it is not necessarily what the reunion was intended to achieve. This was true for Adrian who, as a person of mixed ethnicity, had a particular reason for wanting to know more about his background.

Not everyone finds things they have in common with their birth mother. As ever, it is worth being as clear as you can from the start about your expectations or what you want from the reunion. If initially you think you are just looking for information from your birth mother, then you could try to explain that when you make your initial approach. For example, you might say something like 'I would like to meet up as a chance for me to find out a little more about my background'. The reunion might then develop from there, but if you find that you do not have anything in common, as sometimes occurs, then you will not have raised the other person's expectations too much or made promises that are difficult to keep. Or you might go into the reunion with the hope of establishing a relationship but not find any real connection. Whatever your initial hopes, it is worth trying to maintain some connection, even if it is an occasional letter, postcard, birthday or Christmas card. At some later stage, you might find that you want to renew the contact.

Overloading

In a very small number of cases, reunion runs into difficulty or even breaks down. Emotional needs or even emotional demands, by one side or the other, become too much for the new relationship to bear. This 'overloaded' state is at the extreme end of the reunion scale. As Guy puts it, the reunion had taken over his life and he had placed enormous demands on his birth parents:

> **"**Everything got very much out of perspective and I was throwing myself into this with one hundred percent and giving nothing to anybody else and because of that my marriage collapsed, because of that I had to move. I just ended up in a really crap situation. I just thought this has taken over my life and I've lost an awful lot because of it. But they [birth parents] were the only people there and I kicked at them because of that. They put up with as much as they could and then they had enough, which was fair enough. It reached a point where we couldn't carry on so we just didn't contact each other for ages and ages. Everything I say seems to make everything worse so I've just stopped saying anything. But I thought they'd be able to take me on board come hell or high water and I didn't realise how much I was pushing them. I went to their limit of what they would put up with. And I think if I'd just gone back to where I had been living and sort of seen them whenever it was convenient and all those sort of usual scenarios, it would have been a lot easier. But I instantly needed to depend on them. They were nice friendly looking people and I instantly needed them.**"**

The situation with which Guy was presented was difficult. Reunions where both birth parents have stayed together and then married might sound like an easier option but, in practice, they can sometimes be more complicated. For the adopted person it might seem that a ready-made family exists, with full brothers and sisters, ready to take you in. However, the fact that your parents had stayed together, but without you, may increase your feelings of rejection and a lost sense of what might or should have been. It can also be complicated for the birth parents who might have feelings of guilt about the child who was given up and then never thought about or mentioned to younger siblings.

Guy's story also highlights the importance of only setting out looking for a reunion when things feel relatively good and stable in your life (see Chapters 2 and 3). Other relationships and activities in your life remain important once the reunion gets underway as they help you keep a sense of proportion. A reunion might seem like the answer to your prayers, particularly if you are feeling vulnerable. The temptation might be to give up everything else in your life to pursue it. But in most cases, although you have a blood tie, the relationship is initially too fragile to ask too much of it. If you do find yourself in a very intense reunion where things feel out of control, and you are only seeing and talking to your birth mother, then it is vital to get help. We strongly recommend that you talk to an experienced counsellor and make sure you get the support you need.

Going through phases

We have just described some of the different stages or phases that reunions can go through – some relatively common, others, like overloading, relatively rare. In some reunions a style of relating is established at the start and it continues, but it is important not to think that if you get into a difficult, uncomfortable or unsatisfying way of relating that it will always be like that. Lots of reunions go through all kinds of strange twists and turns, some for the better, some for the worse.

We end this chapter by offering three longer stories about reunions. They are good examples which capture the full range of emotions that people might experience, as well as the different states or stages we have described and how people manage to work through them.

Jessica's reunion

[A three-year reunion initiated originally by her birth mother through an intermediary service but where several years passed before the first meeting.]

"It was my suggestion that we meet up. I think she felt that I wanted to be in control and she was very understanding of that, she never pushed it – she let me lead the whole way. It was quite awkward to start with but also very exciting as well – difficult to explain – to see what you look like. I can't even really remember what we talked about. I just remember afterwards feeling absolutely exhausted . . . We went through various stages – after that first meeting we met up a couple of times, and then I started feeling very stand-offish, I started to feel a bit guilty about my adoptive parents and I only see them probably three or four times a year. I thought 'hang on, I've seen her three times in six weeks' and then I started feeling very uncertain about where it was all going. I thought 'she can't replace my parents – how does she fit into my life? I've satisfied my curiosity now and I know what she looks like and I know all the circumstances surrounding my adoption – is that enough?' I went through a stage then of not answering the phone. It was a real cooling-off period – I think she was very aware of that and she wasn't pushy about it at all. I was worried that she was going to want to be very much a part of my life and I was going to lose control of the situation. I know now that she's had an awful lot of counselling over the years and she was obviously very, very careful and didn't want to upset anything that was happening and yet probably trying to hold herself back – she really wanted it to progress. She made it clear to me that there was nothing she particularly wanted from me and she understood when I said 'my parents are my parents – my brothers are my brothers' – she wasn't trying to impose on that or take me away from them by any means. So she really did all the right things and it was me feeling that I wanted to slow it all down. I wrote to her and explained that I needed some breathing space. She was great, she wrote back and said she understood that. So for the best part of a year we had very little contact, I wrote to her a couple of times, we didn't talk on the phone at all, she sent me postcards – nothing deep at all. So then I thought it would be nice to see her again. I think I phoned her up or something. I think what I wanted to happen, really, was I wanted all the awkward part and the getting to know her part to be over with, and for us to just move on to being friends without having to go through all the difficult conversations. I just wanted to skip all that. I remember explaining that to her and she said 'whatever contact you want to have with me it's fine by me'. And in fact it's really good now –

and I think that's why, it has got to the stage now where I feel completely comfortable ringing her up and we see each other fairly regularly and I really enjoy seeing her. I feel we've got through all the difficult conversations and I've also met a lot of her friends and my family and get on really well with them. I think I've realised that we have so much in common it's unbelievable. We just get on very well. There's definitely a bond there – but I think she feels it more than I do – sometimes she'll say about how much I mean to her and everything and I just feel a bit awkward, a bit slushy. Sometimes I think I don't necessarily want to know how strongly she feels about me, but I do feel good about knowing that I've changed her life. **"**

Phillipa's reunion

[A five-year reunion initiated by Phillipa.]

"It took a little time for me to really feel a connection with her – and Barbara wanted to be my mother again. I had to sit her down and explain 'I have a mother' – and she was sorry that she couldn't be there when I got married, she couldn't be there when I had my children, and shared experiences that she wanted to share with me. That's all in the past and we can't form a relationship on that. I'd rather be very good friends. The bond will re-attach itself in time. She couldn't take the place of my adoptive mother just like that – I said to her 'that's not what I'm looking for'. It was hard for her but she understood straight away that it couldn't happen that easily. . . . Every weekend I'd be at my birth mother's house and in hindsight I was there too much. We didn't give each other enough space. We went through a lifetime's emotions in two or three years. The hurt, the anger, the love, the pain and everything – we said awful things to each other and the following week it would be all lovey-dovey. It really knocked us for six. There was this sudden burst of emotions – and her wanting to take over and both of us wanted to be in control. I went through a stage of really quite despising her – and very, very angry with her for wanting to be this new mother when, really, she had given up the right to be my mother – and just always trying to be there at things where she had no right being. And I'm sure she felt the same sometimes towards me. The emotions of going through a lifetime's relationship with your mother in five years – that's been very tough and that isn't something I was ever pre-warned about – not necessarily the fault of anybody, it's just something that isn't known, all these emotions in such a short space of time. I thought once I'd found her and we'd met life would just go on and everything would all be run-of-the-mill. All awful lot of give-and-take – a bit more giving. I felt an awful lot was being expected of me. I couldn't be myself when we were in social gatherings it was still 'what did you feel?', 'what was it like?' – and I think by then I felt 'forget that bit we want to get on with our relationship'. But the relationship just sort of took off and we are at a happy medium now. Apart from the fact that she's in New Zealand now, and I'm here, but she rings every week and we are far happier now at this level. I would just say just go into it open-mindedly – don't expect too much. Anything you find out it's a bonus. It's something I needed to do – something I had to do and for me, luckily, it's just been absolutely fabulous. **"**

Jacob's reunion

[A 10-year reunion initiated by Jacob.]

❝I can't actually remember what we talked about or what happened in those first few hours. I think I was just so emotional about it all – I wasn't really taking anything in, it was just such an amazing time. To have answers to all these things – I just kept thinking to myself 'this is the first time I've ever met anyone that I share blood with'. It was totally mutual, that kind of wonder – for different reasons of course but the sense of wonder, sense of excitement was very similar. But then we are very, very similar people – we act in similar ways to a lot of different things. We just developed from there, it was obvious at that stage, of course, that we were going to keep in contact, at least for the foreseeable future. It was very intense yeah. I think because we are so alike. But things changed. So many things I think. There are emotions that are very, very strong and are very raw – even after all this amount of time. We went on holiday and I wasn't very nice to Jenny – I was treating her quite badly and when she left I just broke down in tears about how I'd been awful. Our baby was five months old at that stage – it was the first time I'd been with Jenny intensely since I'd felt what it was like to be a parent – so I'd felt a huge resurgence of emotion which simultaneously led me to sympathy for how awful it must have been to have given up a child but being totally unable to understand how anybody could give a child up. Suddenly things that she'd said about how difficult it was, they didn't seem real any more. Whether it's true or not in reality is a different thing altogether, that's what my emotions said. They said 'you can't actually forgive her really'. But I ended up behaving badly and then breaking down in tears because I felt the push from both sides. I've come closer to my adoptive parents as a result of having my daughter. My reaction is to push away my natural family and want to be close to my mother and father who brought me up. I can feel sorry for Jenny but my main emotional identity would now be how my mum and dad felt bringing me up. So I feel a deep bond with them. . . . If you'd asked me five years ago I'd have said I think it's all sorted, but there are dimensions that keep coming up, and I think having a family myself is the one that's caused the biggest changes now, certainly. It's not settled yet – it's a bit up and down. Jenny looked after my daughter last week and she wants to be very involved with her. So it's wonderful for her and wonderful for us – but where does that leave my mum? So I suppose those are the main things that are going on that I've not quite resolved yet. It feels unstable now. I think having a child perhaps it's the anger, I guess, it's been fuelled by the anger – I'm not so angry that I'm going up and shouting at her. . . . She would never reject me – she would never reject me, I feel that totally. It's just that she'll call me her son in the same way as the other children and I know it's not that, not quite. That's what I'm aware of. Its taken eight or nine years. So that's why I say 'unstable' is the word that sums up my situation now – I'm not quite sure where I want it to go – I kind of know where she is really, I know her quite well and I know what her main agendas are I think, I know that she's not a false person, she's a very genuine person but she's not perfect. Yeah it gets more complicated – I'm not quite sure why – I think it's because as one gets older you aim to see implications of what you do more, so I might pick up on subtler things that are important but I wouldn't have noticed 5 years or 10 years ago – so maybe that. It may be the fact that lives get more complicated – as we get older we tend to become part of a more intricate web, rather than being at the bottom of the web we are actually in the middle of one – you can't exist independently then. **"**

Summary

- Birth mother reunions can often be the most difficult type of reunion because of the strong emotions surrounding motherhood. Because of this they can also be the most rewarding and long-lasting.

- There is no set pattern for reunions with birth mothers. Every reunion will be unique. Most reunions though will go through different stages, some easier than others. You may end up feeling closer to your birth mother, or less close, than you did at the beginning. The different states or stages in reunions that we have described might give you some ideas of what sorts of things to expect in your own reunion. Or, if you are already in a reunion, then we hope that our description of different types of reunions and different phases might help to make sense of where you are and possibly how you could try to change things if you need to.

- You and your birth mother might both feel that you have to be on your best behaviour at the start of the reunion. You will both want the reunion to work. Try to avoid the trap of idealising your birth mother or putting her on a pedestal where she can do no wrong; and don't feel that you always have to be the perfect child. As you become more confident in the relationship with each other you will be able to see the other's weak points as well as best points. There may be some arguments and making up on the way (as with Phillipa), and you may not always like the person as much as you initially thought. But you are likely to emerge from the other side with a more real and much stronger relationship, a bit like teenagers quarrelling with their parents to establish their independence (see Chapter 9 for further discussion).

- To make the relationship work it can help to talk about what it means to you and how you would like it to be. These can be difficult conversations at times, especially if you have different expectations or priorities. However, if things do not feel right then the chances are that they will not simply get better by themselves. Sometimes it can be easier to say what you want to say in a letter rather than on the phone or face-to-face.

- On the other hand, after a while and when things are sorted out, do not feel that you always have to talk about the relationship. Just get on and enjoy it!

- You may well be in a situation where one of you places more importance on the reunion than the other. As long as you are up front with each other this need not be a major problem (see Jessica's story).

- You might find yourself behaving in ways with your birth mother that would not occur with anyone else – for example, being 'difficult' or 'unreasonable'. This is not because you are a bad person but is likely to come from the strong feelings of loss, fear of rejection and anger that reunions can generate. If you are finding it hard to move through this period, then be kind to yourself rather than hypercritical. Try to understand why you are acting and feeling the way you are. A friend or counsellor may be able to help you with this. Once you have made sense of your involvement you are at least halfway to doing something about it.

- Relationships are two-way things. You might have a birth mother as sensitive and as thoughtful as Jessica (see above), making working out the relationship much easier. Or you may have a birth mother who is also caught up in the emotion of the reunion. If so, you might have to be the one who does more of the steering and working out of the relationship.

- Make sure that you maintain other relationships and other parts of your life as much as possible during the reunion. This will help you to keep your feet on the ground, keep you in touch with your usual sources of support and stop you investing everything you have into the reunion.

- This chapter has focused on the birth mother relationship, but there are other key players that are likely to influence how the reunion evolves – your own partner/children, your adoptive family, and other birth relatives. Some may offer support, or may want to interfere, or may feel left out of the reunion, and we shall look at these relationships in later chapters.

- This is a long and possibly daunting list of things to think about! But there are two final points that you should bear in mind. (1) No matter what the outcome, most people find the reunion ultimately to be a helpful and consolidating experience. (2) The reunion is likely to be an emotional rollercoaster with highs and lows but it can ultimately be, as Philippa said, 'absolutely fabulous'.

Reunions with birth fathers

5

Fewer people set out initially to search for their birth father and quite often when people look for him, it is as a second step after they have had a reunion with their birth mother.

Introduction

The popular image of adoption reunions, in films or on TV programmes, usually involves birth mothers, and sometimes brothers or sisters. Birth fathers tend not to get much of a mention. This popular image reflects in part what happens in real life, but in detail, the reality is different. In this chapter we look at how many people search for birth fathers and the reasons why.

In the second half of the chapter we see how birth father reunions work out. As with birth mother reunions, there is a wide range of outcomes. Some of the challenges dealt with are similar to those met with birth mothers, including the issue of clarifying roles and expectations. Others are more specific to birth fathers. The overall message is that for most people the birth father reunion is not always as significant as that with their birth mother, but it can still be important and, for some people, more so than with birth mothers. The other main point before we begin is that birth fathers have sometimes had a bad press, occasionally from birth mothers and often in the adoption records. This negative image has prevented some people from beginning a search. We stress in this chapter that an open mind should be kept, not least because the negative images may not be true but also because many adopted people have said that a reunion with their birth father has given them a sense of both sides of their genetic background. And, in quite a few cases, good relationships have developed.

Searching and not searching

Overall, there are fewer reunions with birth fathers than with birth mothers or birth siblings on their maternal side. In our research we found that 73 per cent sought and managed to find their birth mothers, 51 per cent met a brother or sister (more often than not from their mother's side), but only 24 per cent had a reunion with their birth father. Part of the reason why there are fewer birth father reunions is that, in some cases, little or no biographical information is available. Sometimes the birth father is not named on the birth certificate or adoption records and sometimes the birth mother is unable or unwilling to give information about him.

Lack of information is only one reason for the lower rate of birth father reunions. For most adopted people the key figure is the birth mother. We found that 91 per cent of people set off initially to find her. Also, just as fewer adopted people seek their birth father compared to their birth mother, so too do fewer birth fathers than mothers look for their adopted children. The results of our own survey found that of the birth relatives who approached the adoption for information and possible contact, 71 per cent were mothers, 23 per cent were siblings, and only 3 per cent were fathers.

In many ways the approach to adoption search and reunion reflects wider attitudes towards mothers and fathers and to the distinctiveness of the mother–child bond. Kim, who had had a reunion with her birth mother but had chosen not to meet her birth father, reflects a view among some of our interviewees about the differences between mothers and fathers. She raises doubts about what being a father might mean beyond the act of conception, something that she contrasts with maternal care:

> **"**I know that my birth mother, she's thought about me every day since she had me adopted, he probably gives me a thought once every couple of years. You know, the lucky escape probably! Emotionally, looking at it objectively, you're going to get far more from your mother than you ever are from a father.**"**

Kim's speculations were also echoed by Lawrence:

> **"**If I remember back I only thought about tracing my mother. I think maybe because subconsciously there is more of a bond to the mother because she's actually given birth to you, hasn't she. And she was the one, I was told when I was a child that she didn't really want to give me up. I don't think the birth father was ever brought into it.**"**

Some of the reason for this focus on the birth mother might reflect what the adoptive parents might have said and how information has been presented. Inevitably, most of the information available on the adoption record is about the birth mother, although some records will have details about a birth father if, at the time, he was known and actively involved in the decision. However, for many people, it is more than that. As Lawrence points out, the birth mother will have carried the child for nine months and often had some form of brief relationship over the first six weeks. And critically, it is the mother who made the decision to place her child for adoption. She is therefore the parent able to answer two key questions: 'Who am I?' and 'Why was I given up for adoption?'

In comparison, the involvement of birth fathers in most cases will have been much more limited. Some might not even have known about the child, or may have known but chosen not to support the mother in keeping the child. As ever, however, that is not the whole story. While some fathers might not have wanted to be involved, others will have wished to keep the child but the birth mother or her family might have overruled him.

Also, birth fathers, unless they were married to the child's mother, were given no rights to be consulted or have a say in the adoption process.

Delayers and non-searchers

For some people, a relative lack of interest in or curiosity about their birth father continues into adulthood, even after having a reunion with their birth mother. Colin, for example, like several others, had 'never felt inclined to search for my natural father' and reported feeling less inclined after having met his birth mother. Similarly, Nicola told her birth mother that she would not search for her birth father and had planned to search for him only if her birth mother had died.

As well as the reasons mentioned above, this lack of interest can be based on a perception of the birth father as the villain of the piece, having abandoned the mother in her hour of need. Sometimes this was based on how the adoptive parents had told the story. Thelma, for example, said 'I just blamed him and thought "he's a pig" and that was that'. Hilary had always thought that her birth father was a 'cad'. Negative pictures of the birth father might also come from what was reported in the birth records information. The picture painted in the adoption record of Pam's birth father certainly influenced her decision not to search:

> 66 The picture of my father was pretty dire. He was a bit of a waster and an older man. I suppose I'm more interested in my natural mother than my natural father. So he's not quite as significant I suppose or what happened to him. I haven't got a particular desire to meet him. 99

But it is important to remember that the information held in the adoption record may not necessarily be accurate. We made this point in Chapter 2 about the validity of adoption record information. We advise that information about the birth father should be treated with particular caution. Most fathers were not interviewed as part of the adoption process and the information given about him was often hearsay, based on what the birth mother or birth grandparents said. As few birth fathers got the chance to put their side of the story, it is important to keep an open mind when getting information about him, or indeed, when you meet and talk with other birth relatives. Your birth father may have seen things differently from what others say. Wendy's reaction to reading the adoption record is:

> 66 I wanted to kill him! Because I did feel that my birth mother had had an awfully raw deal, but as I was thinking that I was saying to myself 'this is quite a reaction, because you really don't know the full story'. But it did seem to be a very typical situation: that she'd been abandoned by somebody. 99

Quite often the circumstances of the adoption are presented or perceived as a battle between two sides, with the birth mother in one camp and the birth father in the other.

Some people feel a greater sense of loyalty to the birth mother as the 'wronged party', let down by a 'feckless father'. The greater loyalty to the birth mother means that some people explicitly take their birth mother's side and decide to reject their birth father by not searching for him:

> ❝I know his name. As far as I'm concerned he did the dirty on her so I don't even want to know him. You know I'm very, very sympathetic with my mother, I feel dreadful for the situation she was in, you know you really have to be realistic about these things and put yourself in their shoes, I mean she was so young nobody wanted to know, nobody gave a damn, just about reputations. So he didn't give a flying whatever for her, so I don't in turn give a flying . . . for him.❞

Understandably, some birth mothers who believe they had suffered a raw deal feel threatened by the prospect of their newly arrived son or daughter going on to look for the man who had let her down. Although some birth mothers are happy to support and even facilitate their child's search for the birth father, others still feel angry about how they had been treated by the birth father all those years ago. They covertly or overtly discourage a search. As Kim said of her birth mother: 'She spends a lot of time talking about Jim and how he ruined her life and what she'd like to do to him if she saw him again.'

Managing the relationship between the birth mother and father can be a little like children caught up in a difficult divorce where the child's loyalties are divided. Although some adopted people might like to contemplate looking for their birth father, a concern about how this might impact on the newly established relationship with the birth mother can rule out a search. Wendy, whose initial reaction to the adoption record was to be very critical of her father, nonetheless recognised that he might well see things differently. But hearing both sides of a story can be difficult to take on board and challenge newly established loyalties. She had decided not to search for him:

> ❝There's part of me would like to meet him because there are two sides to every story. I would like to hear his version of events. But when you start thinking about it Ireland's a long way away. It's five or six years that my birth mother and I have been together – it's been a lot to come to terms with. You are going to open another set of wounds or you are going to open another Pandora's Box. And in the back of my mind I know I will hear things about my birth mother that I probably don't want to hear and then I've got to spend time coming to terms with them – and I don't really think I want to deal with that. At the moment I feel it's probably best left alone – but if somebody came along to me and said 'we've found him' that would be different.❞

In summary, a few people who have a reunion with their birth mother decide not to pursue a reunion with their birth father. For others, he only becomes real when they read about him in the adoption record. However, the adoption record information, and possibly the response of the birth mother, can mean that some decide not to pursue him, partly feeling that he possibly has little to offer, and partly out of loyalty to the birth mother. If you are at the stage of thinking about whether or not to search for your birth father, we would encourage you to keep an open mind. The information you have about him is unlikely to coincide with what he might say about his behaviour or commitment at the time. It may be even less of a guide to what he might have to offer you now. He may or may not have behaved badly in his youth, but everyone makes mistakes they later regret, even if the consequences were devastating at the time. Equally, he may have had as little control over the situation at the time as your birth mother. It may be worth giving him a chance to put his side of the story. Even if you don't establish a relationship, you may get an opportunity to find out about the other half of your background, helping you fill out the picture of who you are and where you are.

Searching and finding

When a search is made, in some cases it is in the hope of establishing a relationship, in others the birth father represents the final piece of the jigsaw, the final stage of the search for 'roots'. Lucy, for example, was planning a search 'to get it off my list really, get it off my "to do" list and see him – that physical thing is quite important'.

However, although the general pattern is for people to begin by searching for their birth mother, in some circumstances the situation is reversed and the initial search or reunion begins with the birth father, for a number of reasons. The information on the adoption record might mean that tracing the birth father is a much simpler task than finding the birth mother. Sometimes the adoption records indicate that the birth father had wanted to keep the child (and marry the mother) but she had wanted to go ahead with the adoption. Or it could be that the birth mother has died or she has rejected contact and reunion (see below and Chapter 8 for more on this latter group).

There is, however, one particular group of people for whom a search for the birth father can be inherently *more* important than that for the birth mother. For people of mixed race, with a white mother and a black father, a reunion with the birth father is the main way of finding out about their black roots and identity. Una, for example, set out to find her black father long before she contemplated a search for her white mother. She explains it this way:

> ❝It places you – because even though you know that your mother is English and that you are mixed parentage – it still doesn't explain where your blackness comes from and that's what makes you whole then, when you actually know where that does come from. Because it meant that I could then start to get involved in the culture that I knew I was actually from, and not just other people's culture. It grounded me, so I could then focus on the fact that I'm Ghanaian: 'I'm going to find out about my history and my country, I'm going to find out about the food . . .' you know . . . everything . . . That's not negating that my mother was English in any way but you have that side of you all the time because you live in this country so you don't need that side of you being supported because it's there – you've got that all the time. It's the other side that's not supported and viewed as a positive thing when I was growing up – so I think it just balanced the two for me, really. Just gave me a springboard, confidence . . .❞

Regardless of whether the search for the birth father is the first or second stage, it is just as important to make the approach as carefully and as sensitively as it is with birth mothers (see Chapter 3). In our study, people who had already reunited with their birth mother and siblings on their mother's side tended not to use an intermediary when contacting their birth father. People said they felt 'old hands' at doing reunions and did not need as much help, but do not forget that for your birth father it will be his first experience of contact and reunion. He is likely to need preparation.

Searching and finding: the reality

For those who do make contact with their birth father, how do the hopes and expectations match with the reality? The findings of our study revealed that only 3 per cent of birth fathers who were contacted rejected the initial approach by the adopted person (this compares to 9 per cent of birth mothers). However, for the majority who had a successful search, the frequency of contact and the durability of the reunion with their birth father were a little less than with the birth mother, but not appreciably so. For example, 53 per cent of searchers were still in touch with their birth fathers five years after reunion, compared to 69 per cent of birth mothers.

Beyond the statistics, as with birth mothers (and as we shall see with birth siblings), the actual experience of the reunion with birth fathers varies. We shall look in turn at those reunions that ended very quickly, and at some of the reasons for that, then go onto to look at reunions that worked out well.

One-offs

Although proportionately fewer fathers than birth mothers appear to reject initial approaches, there was a higher percentage of birth father reunions that petered out fairly quickly (13 per cent of adopted people lost contact within a year of reunion compared to 6 per cent of birth mother reunions). Harry, one of our interviewees, had had a very positive and intense reunion with his birth mother but felt no emotional connection to his father. He said he did not take to him though he was pleased to have completed the jigsaw:

> ❝I could tell he was me dad. But he was very strange in a way and real spiv type, very strange, not comfortable. I didn't contact him for a while after that and he didn't bother contacting me. No, he hasn't bothered and I thought well I'll leave it a bit longer to see if he does bother to contact me. He didn't. And that was the last. I didn't bother contacting again . . . But I'm pleased I did it. It's laid the ghost to rest so to speak and now I know. It probably makes me work even harder to be the opposite to what he is, or was I should say.❞

Is there a higher cessation rate with birth father contacts because the father is just a difficult person, or are other factors involved? We speculate that in some cases there might be an element of adopted people feeling greater loyalty towards, or being protective of, their birth mother. This might just tip the balance away from a desire to continue contact. This was certainly an issue that Jacob considered, having also had a very intense reunion with his birth mother:

> "I met him and then didn't pursue it. He was quite happy to meet me and we had several meetings and several days and he was nice enough but I just didn't like him very much really, I think. I don't know quite whether that was because I'd had my vision of him coloured already, because of what my birth mother had said, or what he had done – deserted – or whether I just didn't like him. And I think it was because I just didn't like him, because I wasn't judging anybody at that stage. I wouldn't have judged him until I had some experience of him. I wanted him to say 'sorry' I guess and he didn't, maybe that affected it a bit. There was no emotional attachment. I didn't find him a very honourable person. I found after I got to know him a little bit I didn't have a lot of respect for him whereas I had a lot of respect for my birth mother. We just didn't really click. We came from different sides."

Continuing positive contact

Most of our detailed knowledge of birth father reunions comes from the 74 in-depth interviews we conducted as part of our research. We therefore have a number of rich stories of what happened, although the numbers are fairly small. Even so, we can spot some trends. We found three different types of ongoing reunions with birth fathers:

- Where there were separate successful reunions with both the birth mother and birth father.
- Where there had been no birth mother reunion or the reunion had ended.
- Where the birth mother and birth father were still together or had subsequently got back together.

Although the numbers in our research are small, it appears that it can be quite difficult to have equally full independent reunions with both the birth mother and birth father. Very few of our interviewees had as strong a reunion with their birth father if they had previously established a good relationship with their birth mother. However, Patrick, who we met in Chapter 2, was one of the few exceptions. Here is what he says about the reunion with his birth father, three years after first meeting his birth mother:

> "It went very well, got on very, very well. I see him about three times a year, sort of thing. It was nerve-racking, but I think they were more nervous than we were, 'cos I'd met my brother and sister and mother, done it before. He's got three other children. It's quite funny actually he always jokes, he said to me he wonders how many more there are! . . . he's actually quite amusing, he's got quite a good sense of humour fortunately."

There were more examples of stronger birth father reunions where the birth mother had died, had rejected contact, or had been searched for second or, as in Tara's case, where the birth mother reunion was very fraught:

> **"**It's very good. Very, very good, I said to him when we first made contact 'I'm not looking for a relationship I would just like to meet you and whatever happens after will be what happens'. I was always told 'he's not paternal, don't expect too much'. But he's a very spiritual person and said 'I knew you'd find me'. We speak every few weeks. He is very spiritual, very right-on hippyish. We have a jokey relationship. It's fun. I think he was surprised by how much alike we are in personality traits. I don't think he was prepared for that. I suppose the bonus for me is, unlike having what I call 'real parents' I can talk to my father and he can talk to me and feels easy talking to me about things that a traditional father – that you would have grown up with – perhaps wouldn't share and vice versa. **"**

There were also a small number of successful reunions where the birth parents had remained together and the adopted person was able to build a strong relationship with both parents. This was the situation in Ian's case:

> **"**It's really a fairy tale story. I've been very, very lucky. The main gains are I'm probably a better person for it – more stable, my birth parents seem to have gained out of it, it's helped their relationship. The only negative side is my adoptive parents and they seem to have taken it quite badly. They have to accept the consequences as much as I do and they've really got to get used to it, I can't change the way I am, and I can't change the circumstances. **"**

This brief review of the three types of successful birth father reunions highlights some important points. It seems that many people tend to prioritise making a success of the birth mother reunion, leaving them with a sense of loyalty to her that can affect a subsequent birth father reunion. Where the relationship with the birth father is stronger, it tends to be in situations where the reunion with the birth mother has not happened or has not been successful. However, as is the very nature of reunions, there are always exceptions to the pattern.

What made Patrick's reunion with his birth father work where others had not? One thing which came through in Patrick's story was that he did not feel any sense of torn loyalty between his birth mother and birth father. Nor did he feel that either of his parents should be blamed or held responsible for the adoption. Interestingly, Patrick was also one of the few who felt really angry at the social attitudes of the fifties and sixties which frowned upon young, single pregnant women keeping their babies. He was particularly angry at the church and its attitudes. Patrick's feelings make sense. In his mind, placing a child for adoption is contrary to how things are generally supposed to be and people who have been adopted have to find an explanation for why it happened. Quite often adopted people who have developed a strong relationship with their birth mother then find it hard not to blame the birth father in some way for their adoption. This, as we have seen, can obstruct a positive reunion with him. This is not to say that some fathers were not supportive. But recognising the social constraints of the time on both parents, as Patrick did, enabled him to feel free to build positive separate relationships with both birth parents.

Friend or father?

For some, sorting out their relationship with their birth father is straightforward, for others it can be more of a challenge, as with birth mothers. Working out exactly what the birth father–adopted person relationship should look like is not always easy. This is not surprising given that it is being built from scratch in adulthood rather than in childhood. Some people manage it with few problems, as Jenny found:

> ❝The best thing I ever did was to find my father. That first meeting with him changed my life forever. We have a very special relationship. ❞

Other people find themselves dealing with a relationship in which their birth father is under-involved and the adopted person has to make all the running. Then there are reunions where the birth father gets too involved. Getting the balance right or comfortable requires as much negotiation as it does in many birth mother reunions. Equally, establishing a satisfactory relationship depends as much on the attitudes, behaviour and feelings of both the birth father and the adopted person – relationships cut both ways!

Making the running

Some ongoing father reunions run into difficulties. The adopted person feels that he or she is doing all the work to keep the relationship alive, although there is always the potential for confusing messages about whether the relationship is about friendship or the father–child role. This can be especially true in father–daughter relationships. Yasmin, for example, had a very low-key relationship with her birth father and felt frustrated that he made fewer efforts to see her than she did to see him. However, she was not sure what she wanted from him: 'I'm not asking him to be a father, I don't want him to be a father to me.' Cora's experience with her birth father was similar. After an intense honeymoon period she became increasingly frustrated. She felt she was making all the running in the relationship. She was caught between trying to keep contact and also framing the relationship as a friendship:

> ❝I've noticed that it's got more and more difficult because we are very similar and because he's no good at being committed. And I'm very committed and if I keep being committed and I get nothing back then I get pissed off. He's very set in his ways and he thinks that I should always call him and that I'm responsible for it all. For two or three years in a row, at the beginning of the year I wrote him a letter saying 'I would really like to have a relationship with you, I completely understand and accept if you don't want to have a relationship with me, but if you do and I sense that you do, then

it has to be a two-way street, I cannot be the one that is always ringing up to make the arrangements and so on. I know it's difficult for you to hear me say that you can't be my father, you are my biological father and there's no getting away from that, but you are not emotionally my father and you didn't bring me up, but I have deep respect for you and you know, let's think about that later. Let's build a friendship and in order to do that we need to drop the odd line or ring up and leave messages on the answer-phone or whatever.' **"**

For other people, the relationship seems less frustrating, although it can be low-key. Gemma, who had been rejected by her birth mother had just such a low-intensity relationship with her birth father:

"We do send each other Christmas cards, Easter cards, birthday cards, and I have been to visit twice. I felt like a stranger when I met him because of the different situation, 'cos we'd met in a sort of cafe, that's what he wanted, and I felt like I was just someone going to meet someone the counsellor knew and it was strange meeting him. We met again but I don't feel like a daughter because we're not that close. We don't ring each other like daughters do. We don't write like daughters do. **"**

Fending off

The difficulty in trying to work out the father role from scratch is further highlighted in cases where people feel that their fathers are becoming too involved, or even too fatherly. Alison, for example, had chosen to search for her birth father before her birth mother but had then felt overwhelmed by him:

"He kept referring to being my 'father' so I kept saying 'no, you are not my father and under no circumstances must you ever think that you are my father'. And he kept saying 'well, biologically I am'. I said 'biologically you may be – but at the end of the day you are not my father'. He was keen to maintain contact fairly regularly, fairly quickly – it was almost like he wanted to bring me into the fold and I was going to be his 'daughter' – and I was resisting that. So I felt completely overwhelmed, you know, there was this curiosity – so there was a draw to see him – but then also, you know, 'get away' – 'what are you in my life?' I was being a bit unfair on him, but I didn't know what I wanted. **"**

Getting the relationship right

Just as with birth mothers, there are many types of working relationships with birth fathers. Some adopted people want a close relationship and a highly-involved father. Others want a more friendship-based arrangement. This mirrors the low- and high-pitch balances we saw in birth mother reunions (see Chapter 4). But the under- and over-involved birth father reunions just go to show how tricky it can be to strike a good balance, particularly when the adopted person is clear that something closer to friendship than a father–child relationship is being sought. However, the discussions and arguments needed to sort out the character of the contact may mean that you emerge with a stronger and more honest relationship than if you try to dodge these issues or simply allow the reunion to drift in an unsatisfactory or frustrating way.

Given the sensitivities over the fatherhood role, one approach for fathers is to offer friendship rather than presume to be able to take on a father's role. It is a difficult balance to strike, but some birth fathers manage it extremely well, as illustrated in a letter written to one of our interviewees:

> **"**For me to act as your father would be inappropriate and morally wrong but I hope that I can become a friend that loves you very much. If at any time you need a shoulder to cry on or a butt to kick I promise I will be there for you.**"**

Phillipa's birth father showed his commitment without presuming to take on the role of father. As a result, the reunion worked out extremely well.

Summary

- Fewer people sought out their birth fathers than their birth mothers, but reunions with birth fathers can result in contact that is nearly as frequent and durable as contact with birth mothers.

- It may be easy to be given a negative impression of birth fathers from your adoption records or perhaps your birth mother or maternal grandparents. Do not forget that birth fathers were seldom consulted. They might have a different perspective on what should have happened. They are also the only real source of information about the half of your genetic make-up and family background. Try to keep an open mind and, if you wish, find out for yourself.

- Think about what you might want from a reunion with a birth father. Are you really just interested in a photo and family history or would you like to get to know him more? How could you make sure that this message gets across?

- Using an intermediary is just as important for a birth father reunion as with any other reunion.

- For some people the reunion with the birth father can be much more important or long-lasting than that with the birth mother. But where a successful reunion has been built with your birth mother, loyalty to her can make it more difficult to establish a positive relationship with your birth father. Again, try to keep an open mind about his attitudes and behaviour. It is possible to have good relationships with both sides of your family, but it needs sensitive handling.

● Getting the relationship with your birth father right may need just as much work as with your birth mother. Most adopted people seem to start off wanting a good friendship. For some it really helps if birth fathers can fit into the friendship role and at the same time make sure that they are neither over- or under-involved!

● Birth father reunions can be just as emotional and complex and raise as many issues as other reunions. Be prepared for this even if you have already gone through reunions with other birth relatives.

Reunions with birth siblings

The main message of this chapter is that, in many ways, reunions with brothers and sisters can be the easiest and most straightforward to manage.

Introduction

Many adopted people find out during their search that one or both of their birth parents have had other children before or after the adoption. Most people are excited by the prospect of a reunion with a full or half-brother or sister. In this chapter, as with the previous chapters on birth mother and birth father reunions, we look at the variety of ways in which reunions work out with siblings. We begin this chapter by looking at the reasons why sibling reunions tend to be less complicated, then consider some of the particular challenges of sibling reunions and the strategies that people have used to deal with them.

Lowering the pressure

We've already suggested that sibling reunions often work out well and tend to last. In our research 85 per cent of searchers were still in contact with a birth sibling three years or more after the original reunion, compared to 76 per cent still in touch with a birth mother and 70 per cent with their birth father. To give a flavour of a sibling reunion here is Roger's account of his meeting with his sister:

> **"**Yeah we'd been talking on the phone by this time. Yeah I thought about what it would be like – but . . . Oh it was just amazing – I think we were just shell-shocked – I don't think we said anything for about 10 minutes. We hit it off straight away – we very quickly developed a bond with each other. And its probably got stronger – I'm quite close to her. **"**

Of course not all reunions work out so well, but on the whole sibling relationships seem easier and less complicated than reunions with a birth mother or birth father. There seem to be two main reasons why this is so.

First, sibling relationships are usually not so emotionally charged as parent–child relationships. This is generally true of non-adoptive family relationships but also seems to carry through into adoption reunions. That is not to say that sibling bonds cannot be very strong or that sibling reunions will be unemotional, but some of the strong feelings of anger and hurt around issues of loss and rejection that can appear in birth mother and birth father reunions are less likely to be present in sibling reunions. The discovery and experience of meeting a brother or sister seem to generate uncomplicated feelings of curiosity or excitement.

The absence of feelings of anger, loss and rejection may be because brothers and sisters carry no responsibility or blame for either the conception or adoption, unlike mothers or fathers. For some, it is far easier to imagine a reunion with a sibling than with a birth parent, especially a birth mother. One of our interviewees, Barry, had established a very close relationship with his brothers but took several years to finally agree to meet his birth mother, and even then he approached her very cautiously, putting all manner of emotional safeguards and distances between them. The contrast between his joyful embrace of his brothers but caution towards his birth mother may be a need to protect himself from a further rejection by her:

> **❝**I got a letter out of the blue – 'you are the youngest of three brothers'. It was a big shock, but every single one of us get on absolutely famously and have done from the very first instance we met. Peter and I are more or less identical in manners, in behaviour, things like that. The same with Simon. It couldn't possibly have worked out better, everyone just gets on well together. We're just like brothers should be. Not afraid to say anything about anything to each other – just like best friends I suppose . . . But I am going to see the real mother next month for the first time. There's no relationship going to develop out of it. There's not going to be 'oh my long lost mother I'll come and see you every other weekend and you'll come and stop with us for Christmas'. Too far down the line for that. She knows that as well, she's agreed to that. I'm not taking my daughter down to see her – because I don't want her running around saying to her Grandma 'oh I've got another grandma' or anything like that – because that would be upsetting for my parents. I don't feel I want to see her out of any affection I've got for her – because having never met her before in my life, I can't have any affection for the person. [In fact the reunion with his birth mother did turn out to be very positive.]**❞**

Our interviewees were mostly very excited about finding and meeting new brothers or sisters. Some, however, were indifferent about it and were much more focused on their reunion with a birth parent. The lack of the 'complicated' emotions surrounding sibling relationships means that reunions can progress in a more direct fashion. Or, for some people, it means that they are simply not interested in pursuing the reunion.

The second reason why sibling reunions are potentially more straightforward than birth parent reunions, is that society generally has an 'additive' approach to siblings. By that we mean that we are used to people having more than one sibling and sibling groups growing. Siblings often come in multiples. In contrast we are used to people having a single person in the mother or father role. Just as with step-parents, it can, therefore, be more taxing to determine the role the 'extra' (birth) mother or (birth) father should play alongside your existing adoptive mother and adoptive father. And having more than one parent also raises issues of competition and loyalty. These issues are not entirely absent among siblings – in some cases adoptive siblings are worried about being replaced by the birth siblings – but overall they seem much less common and much less difficult than the issues raised by having more than one mother or father.

Getting in and getting on

So far we have highlighted the positive aspects of sibling reunions. As ever, though, there are things that can go wrong and there can be challenges to negotiate. One of the first tasks is to work out whether you like each other or whether you have anything in common.

For most people the reunion with new brothers or sisters seems to go well from the start. By far the most common feelings are those of excitement and anticipation. Dawn, for example, recalled her teenage brothers telling their school friends about her first visit: ' "Ooh our sister's coming down" and people were saying "you ain't got a sister" and they go "we have!" ' The actual reception by brothers and sisters is often described in very positive terms, with frequent reference to 'hitting it off immediately' or 'making me feel at home'. Sometimes this welcome can be exuberant or it can be very laid-back though still reassuring even when siblings have only been told recently about you, their other brother or sister. Brothers, in particular, seem to specialise in the relaxed approach to welcoming, as in Olive's case:

> **“**They are so laid-back about the whole thing. When they first met me it was 'hello sis, hello mum, here's the washing'. And I was so nervous and they just said 'hello' and 'you can tell she owes you 30 years' worth of Christmas presents'. That was their whole attitude. And it was as if I'd been part of the family. I know when my mum had to tell them all she got herself in a complete state, burst into tears and explained what had happened and they just accepted it.**”**

Some sibling relationships are very close and active from the beginning. Una, for example, immediately developed a very strong relationship with her sister, seeing her regularly and phoning several times a week, and described having similar tastes and a similar outlook on life. In these kinds of reunions the newly found sibling is rapidly integrated into the birth family and often the birth siblings are welcomed into the adoptive family.

In other cases the relationship can be broadly positive but not necessarily very active. Paula had a very close relationship with her sister but a more limited one with her brother, saying 'he's thrilled to bits when he sees me but we're not great ones for on the phone every five minutes. He's just got married and got his own life now.'

It is uncommon for there to be hints of dislike or hostility from siblings. Harry's reunion with his brother was very low key:

> ❝I had met my brother and he didn't really want to know. No problems, we'd talk and all the rest of it but he just doesn't really want to know. If he's ever down there when I'm there, great. I think mum had a feeling he perhaps felt threatened that I was always the oldest, here's the older male coming in you know. I can understand it and I've never pushed anything or done anything since. We do get on, there's certainly no hatred or anything now.❞

One of the points that Harry picks up is the impact on the birth order of the sibling group. The arrival of a 'new' brother or sister does usually alter people's perceptions of where they are in the birth order, usually pushing them down one step. This is probably more of an issue for siblings who had thought that they were the oldest child, although it may well be something of which the adopted person is more conscious than the sibling. While a few people worry about this before the reunion, it does not seem to occur very often in practice.

In Harry's case there was some element of competition and unease among the two brothers. However, in our research, it was rare for siblings to be openly hostile to the new sibling. Rochelle's reunion was one of the very few where animosity was expressed:

> ❝I got home and there were all these brothers and sisters. And my coming, in a way, stirred up old resentments, their insecurities and their anger about the way they felt they'd been treated or whatever. My sister treated me really badly for a long time. And I know she's a nice enough girl but there are too many years, too many comments like 'why don't you go back where you came from? If I had another family I wouldn't be coming round here, what do you want these people for? You're not my sister . . . blah, blah'.❞

While the majority of siblings get on well, sometimes extremely well, there are no obvious predictors of who will or will not form the strongest relationships. Sometimes women can get on brilliantly with sisters but are not as close to brothers, or vice versa. In other cases a newly reunited brother and sister might forge a strong relationship while two sisters may not. Nor does it seem to make much difference whether the siblings have known about their brother or sister for a long time or have only recently been told. Sometimes 'direct' sibling reunions, where there are no reunions with a birth parent, can work well, but sometimes they do not really get going. Alternatively, two siblings might have a very strong relationship independent of an equally strong reunion with a birth parent.

The lack of predictability in sibling reunions is probably not that surprising. Although many people are struck by their physical resemblance to their siblings, what also emerges is the importance of whether or not you get on with them or feel you have something in common. Bonds can be strong, but are based very much on 'hitting it off' and then developing the relationship from there. This is most obvious when adopted people are meeting a sibling pair or group. Although good relationships can be forged with all the siblings (as with Stuart mentioned above), it is also common for the incomer to feel closer to one or two siblings rather than to all of them. Indeed, one of the advantages of meeting more than one sibling is the much greater chance of finding at least one sibling with whom you might discover common ground and shared interests. In many ways this is typical of how siblings relate in non-adopted situations – some siblings are closer to each other than others.

On an individual level most sibling reunions work out well. When a sibling is not close, he or she tends not to worry too much if the reunion with other siblings is not particularly well accepted. But where there is just one sibling, the adopted person may worry more if a degree of intimacy cannot be developed. Lawrence reflected:

> **"**I don't know really how I should feel. I mean she phoned me two weeks back and started talking and then there was a silence so I started waffling on about all sorts of things just to try and keep the conversation going. I do feel a little bit awkward with her because we're just not alike. Eventually we'll find a common denominator, we will get a bond, something will happen and we'll just sort of start talking and it'll gradually settle down into it. I guess it would be, it would turn out to be that we've got this good friend who lives in Nottingham. Occasionally we'll go and see her, occasionally she'll come and see us. I wouldn't let it go away and I don't think she would. But there's not this big bond.**"**

Although Lawrence was clearly concerned about the situation, he was realistic enough to give it time to see what happened. While many people are overjoyed to find a sibling with whom they might really connect, it is unlikely to occur in every case. Nevertheless, as with Lawrence, even a low-key relationship can still offer an important link with your roots.

The other potentially difficult area to handle is where a sibling has significant personal difficulties, such as drink or drug problems. Again, this is fairly uncommon, but can happen. We look at this issue in more detail in Chapter 9.

Finding your place

On a one-to-one level there are usually far fewer major problems with birth siblings than with birth parents. However, as the relationship develops, the next question is to work out where you fit within the sibling group and the wider birth family. This area can prove more difficult to manage. Put simply, does the blood tie entitle you to expect to be treated the same as the other brothers and sisters, sons and daughters? Or, does the lack of a shared history mean there will always be differences in how you are treated? Can the adopted person be a full and equal member of the birth family, or will there always be a difference? On an intuitive level most people might think that adopted people should be treated the same as any other son or daughter or brother and sister. Certainly this was the expectation of many of our interviewees. It was often what their birth relatives tried to achieve or felt that they were doing. However, the reality is that the lack of a shared history can mean that almost all adopted people feel some degree of difference, some element of outsideness. This is not necessarily obvious at the beginning of the reunion but becomes more apparent over time. Although the awareness of feeling different is not unusual, there are differences in how people cope. Let us look at this in more detail.

Similarities and differences

For a small number of adopted people, full membership of the birth family is almost impossible as their birth parent (usually birth mother) chooses to keep the reunion hidden from her family. In Gail's case, for example, her birth mother had kept the adoption, and then the reunion secret from all her family. She felt she could not introduce Gail to her siblings. In Tara's case, the reunion with her siblings took place long after the original reunion with her birth mother due to the latter's fears of upsetting her other children. Keeping such a secret is rare but when it does happen, it can feel uncomfortable. In these situations you may feel you have to go along with the birth parent's wishes and hope that you will be able gradually to build trust to the point where she feels able to acknowledge your existence to the rest of the family. Ironically almost all birth siblings who are told about their adopted brother or sister feel excited and intrigued, and wonder why they had not been told earlier.

However, even for the majority who had a positive meeting with their siblings not long after the birth parent reunion, there can still be a sense that they remain different. This can include a feeling that you are not always told about family news, not being invited to every family gathering, or not being contacted as regularly as other sons or daughters. This is such a common experience that we'll give you some examples, beginning with Helen's growing feeling that her birth mother put less effort into contacting her than her siblings:

> **❝**I don't feel as if I belong to them. I did initially. 'Cos she made me feel so welcome and like I said, she'd write and she'd phone and then it got less and less. She wanted me to be treated as a daughter, wanted all the family to treat me the same as the others, yet she couldn't bring herself to phone me any more, I was doing all the phoning all the time. And then I found out when I spoke to my sister that she was ringing her every couple of weeks and I thought 'well why can't she ring me?' She only ever rings me at Christmas or New Year.**❞**

Not being kept fully in the picture can mean that the adopted person misses out on crucial pieces of family news such as an illness and a hospital visit. Tara, for example described this 'not being involved as a family member' as the most difficult aspect of her reunion. Being aware of different rates of contact and degrees of sharing can lead to the perception that other siblings are more favoured. This was Jacob's perception:

> **❝**However much love is professed, as time's gone on I know the difference between us – me and my other natural siblings – if you met my birth mother you'd know what a statement that was really – because she is this earth mother who would be very

shocked by me saying that – but I know, really, that I'm not the same. It's something I might well say at some point, because I could feel in a time of tension that that might come out, because it's something that I've been thinking more as time's gone on. **"**

Dealing with difference

Perhaps a majority of adopted people feel slightly set apart from their brothers and sisters. There is variation in how people respond to the situation, some feeling that it is unfair, some that it is inevitable and understandable. Some people deal with their difference by competing or by hanging back. Others, and this seems to work better, reach a point where they simply have to acknowledge that differences are inevitable given the years they have been living apart. We shall look at each approach in turn.

Dealing with difference by competing

One way of dealing with feeling different from other siblings is to try and compete, to achieve greater closeness to birth relatives in spite of the lack of shared history. Veronica's reunion with her mother and two siblings was complicated. In her case she found one sister to be much more welcoming than the other. There was also a strong sense of her feeling a need to claim her place in the family, perhaps making her more competitive than she might otherwise have been:

"When we first met her husband actually said 'Mary [the birth mother] is more like you than any of the other two, personality wise', he said 'you're so alike' and I think Mary feels that and I think that's why we've got so close so quick. I think it's because I've got more of Mary's personality than Lucy and Jeanette, perhaps we've got an added closeness. But I think it is hard for people in families to see their mothers overjoyed at the long departed. I don't think I'd like it. **"**

Entering a new family can be daunting, particularly when meeting siblings who have lived with your parent since birth. Everyone naturally tries to connect with their 'new' relatives. There is a delicate balance to strike between finding common ground and not threatening to compete with or upset existing relationships. You might meet brothers or sisters who are anxious about you becoming involved with their family. Their worries are as understandable as your need to work out your place. The difficulties that do crop up gradually resolve over time, and everyone begins to settle down and adjust to new patterns, new family rhythms.

Coming to terms

A few people start out with the idea that they will be treated just like the other siblings. Given people's very different histories, this is unlikely. Some people become disappointed and disillusioned, or they feel hurt and rejected when small differences in treatment occur. But most people come to terms with the idea that because they have a different history with another family, there will always be some separateness, some differences that set you slightly apart and preclude full integration with the 'new' family. Memories are different. Customs, habits and rituals vary. For some, the realisation is a painful event, although acknowledged and understood. Wendy explains:

> **❝**We can all make each other laugh, have so much in common and I thought 'I've come home'. These are my people. . . . But up until very recently I used to feel very left out. I wasn't raised with them. I don't know the way they think. I'd say it's taken me over the last year to come to terms with the fact that I will never be as close. My brother got married and my sister was chief bridesmaid and my younger brother was best man – and I wasn't anything. I suppose there's a little niggle there – like 'oh why haven't I been picked?' You have to accept that there are times when you are going to feel the rub. But there are an awful lot of ups. I think the downs actually help you come to terms with things. I've definitely looked at things and thought 'well, why do I feel like this, why do I feel left out?' It's made me think around things a bit more – they owe me nothing, they don't know me. When I'm left out by the children it's painful – it does hurt – and usually it's about something so trivial. And I have learnt to say to myself now – 'what are you getting excited about?'**❞**

Reaching Wendy's level of understanding is not always easy. It had taken her time to come to terms with feeling separate. The small and unintended differences in how she was treated could still hurt, but her expectations had become more realistic. She gradually came to understand that she was a full, albeit different kind of family member.

ADVICE BOX! ADVICE BOX! ADVICE BOX! ADVICE BOX! ADVICE BOX!

Dealing with difference

In spite of everyone's best intentions, it is likely that there will be some differences in how you are seen and treated compared to other siblings who have grown up in your birth family. This can be upsetting, especially when it only slowly dawns on you over time. You will need to find a way to deal with these feelings if the reunion is going to work out. Here are some suggestions to bear in mind:

● Don't take it as a personal rejection, even though it is you who has in effect been singled out. But it is *not* personal, it is just a logical consequence of not growing up in that family. You could never be exactly the same as the other siblings no matter how nice/funny/attractive you are.

▶

- Try to spend time with each family member individually rather than trying to attach to a whole group. In any family there is a group identity, but there are also well-established relationships between individual family members. You are likely to feel more part of the whole if you are comfortable with each member, and if they are comfortable with you. This might also help to reassure some siblings who are feeling a bit threatened by your arrival.

- Think about whether you really want to be treated just like the other siblings. Being different means that you might miss out on some good bits of family life, but it might also mean that you don't always have to take on all the hard family tasks.

- Be realistic. In all families there are some members who are closer than others. All parents relate to each child as an individual. Give yourself and your new family members time to work out how you all fit together. You may find that you see some regularly, others hardly at all. This happens in most families.

- Don't forget that you also have another family – your adoptive family. Most people still have stronger or even stronger connections with their adoptive family after a reunion (see Chapter 7). As Kenneth says 'I always call her my mother now. I'm part of the family but not right in it because she has got her own family and I've got my own family. She calls me her son. My brothers treat me as a brother.'

- You may want to talk to some family members about how you are feeling. Try not to make it sound like an accusation, putting people on the defensive and making them feel guilty.

Hanging back

Having described how most people feel when they experience being treated differently, there are cases when the situation is reversed. The adopted person finds it hard to accept being a full member of the family. Sometimes the birth parent makes a real effort to treat each sibling the same, and the family accepts you as a full member. This can cause some discomfort if you don't feel entitled to this status. Cheryl said:

> ❝The saddest part about it is that my birth father's made every effort, even down to stupid things like 'I've changed my will to include you'. I don't care, but I think he felt

it was a way of saying 'look you do exist, you are my daughter, I'll show you somehow'. For a long time I pushed him away, a long long time, years. I felt I didn't need him. And from their point of view I'm not novelty any more which is quite good because it means that you are just part of it all. But at a family funeral I found myself in the car following the hearse and I thought 'hang on I'm not supposed to be here, I'm not important enough to be here'. And at the grave, I did pull right back and stood out of the way. Sometimes I feel I'm where I shouldn't be, I don't feel I have the right to be there. They felt I did. I felt I didn't. **"**

Where it is clear that full membership is being offered, this can feel a little overwhelming at first. There can be many reasons for such a reaction. It might be that you are being offered more than you bargained for, or you might feel that you are somehow betraying your adoptive family, or you might still fear that rejection might lurk somewhere down the line and so you do not want to fully commit yourself, at least not yet. Give yourself time to find your place. You will learn when to become fully involved and when to step back. Olive provides a good example when, in spite of a very positive reunion with her birth mother and siblings, she thought it wise not to 'interfere' in family problems, saying: 'I'm still treading a little bit carefully and I probably always will.'

Summary

- Sibling reunions are often the most emotionally straightforward of all types of adoption reunions. They tend to last, often with fairly high rates of contact.

- Most siblings seem to welcome their new-found brother or sister even if they have only recently heard about them, although some siblings will not be very interested.

- Although sibling reunions are relatively problem-free, it is quite common for adopted people to build a stronger relationship with one or two siblings rather than with all of them.

- One of the few real issues in sibling reunions is whether or not the person is treated just like any other brother or sister. Although some people expected or were promised that they would be treated no differently from any other son or daughter, in reality this is difficult to achieve, simply because they had not grown up together. Some people find this disappointing, even a little hurtful, but given very different family histories, most people understand it could hardly be otherwise.

The adoptive family and reunion

Whether and how the adoptive family is involved can be one of the most sensitive parts of the search and reunion process.

Introduction

Search and reunion is mainly about making a link between an adopted person and members of that person's original birth family. But in most cases the *adoptive* family is also important in how the search and reunion process unfolds and how it all works out. Many adopted people worry about hurting their adoptive parents by telling them about a search for their 'other family' or 'other parents'. At the same time, however, it can also feel wrong to conduct the search in secret. One of the key tasks of this chapter is to look at this dilemma of telling or not telling. In the first half of the chapter we shall look at the pros and cons of telling adoptive parents about the search or reunion. We shall then outline the various approaches that adopted people use and explore how these develop. In the second half of the chapter we shall move on beyond the initial stages of reunion to look at how the relationship with the adoptive family may be influenced over the longer term and the different ways in which people strike a balance between contact with their adoptive and birth families.

To tell or not to tell?

One of the key questions facing anyone thinking about a search or reunion is the question of whether or not to tell your adoptive parents. Sometimes this issue will be very easy to resolve. In some families adoption is a topic that has always been talked about freely and the adoptive parents will have already given clear messages that they would support any search for the birth family. These are the parents who are comfortable about your search, indeed they may even have encouraged you. They are typically told at an early stage during or even before the search.

For most people adoption is a topic that has been too sensitive to talk about to any great extent, as we saw earlier in Chapter 2. This means that in many cases it is hard to predict how the adoptive family might react to your wish to search. Most adopted people assume that their parents will feel betrayed or threatened. But not telling them about the search means that you are doing it behind their backs. The dilemma is whether to let parents know and risk them feeling upset, threatened or rejected (and possibly rejecting you in turn), or not to tell and risk that they might find out later while you, in the meantime, lead a double life.

No one can tell you what will be best in your circumstances. There are many factors that can influence what might happen – including the strength of your relationship with your adoptive parents. Having heard about many different reunions we would, on balance, encourage you to seriously consider telling your parents about the search. Obviously we cannot guarantee that it will work out, or that it is the best solution in the long or short term. But there are lots of reasons why we think it might be the best way forward.

First, the evidence from our study clearly shows that most people do tell their parents at some stage, and in most cases this works out well. We found almost three-quarters of adopted people told their parents about the search, although only just over half told adoptive siblings. Only 21 per cent did not tell anyone about their search and reunion.

The second reason is about being open and honest. A prime reason for telling your adoptive parents about a search or reunion is because it feels an important thing to do that can not really be kept a secret. Although we believe that parents generally should be told, it does not mean that they will not feel anxious, even a little hurt, as Zara discovered:

> **❝**They found it difficult – not hurtful but they found it difficult – they wanted to help me but it was very hard for them. But my mum gave me the number here for the adoption agency. So that's what I did and went along to see my records. I then went to see Mum because I didn't want to hide anything from them. They know everything. I'm mature enough now to understand that they just want what's best, and they didn't want to see me hurt. So I thought I don't want to hurt them and keep them in the dark about things. I told them that I'd received my records and I was going to go up that weekend and I said I'll bring the records up and you can have a look as well – and told them quite openly over the phone.**❞**

A third reason for telling is simply that saying nothing is not necessarily a safer or an easier option. The secrecy surrounding adoption and the difficulty in talking about it puts adopted people who want to search in a double bind where there could be potentially negative consequences. While it might seem risky to tell and deal with the consequences of telling, so too is not telling. Once a search, and especially a reunion has started, it is very difficult to maintain the secret, especially if you have children who might inadvertently 'spill the beans'. Adoptive parents who find out about a reunion second-hand or by accident can be as upset by the way they found out about the reunion as about the reunion itself. The difficulties of living a double life and dealing with the aftermath of being found out are captured eloquently by Jacob:

> **❝**I lied. There's quite a lot of lies went on. Or distortions. I might be honest about where I was going but I wouldn't say about details. If I was required to give details I'd

have to lie a bit. It wasn't a comfortable thing to do and it got worse. A dual life is not very good. My adoptive mother found out a couple of years afterwards and was pretty devastated. If you were to ask her she would give you that it was more the way she found out than the fact that I'd done it. And there's a lot of game plan still about how it's 'all right'. But it isn't really. **"**

A final reason for telling is to get your parents' emotional permission or 'blessing' to proceed. The importance of having the support and 'emotional permission' of your adoptive parents cannot be underestimated. Alison, for example, was thrilled by her adoptive mother's response:

"I did talk about it to my mum and she was quite supportive and that and I can remember getting to be nearly 18 and it was my mum that actually said to me, 'look why don't you ask the social worker to see if she can get some information for you?', and that just felt like it was so much support from my mum. I thought this is brilliant. You know that she's being cool about it. **"**

The advantage of this approach is that it took the pressure off Alison. She had been given emotional permission to search by her adoptive mother and was then able to share the information she had obtained with her mum. Not all adoptive parents are able to offer such a strong endorsement but, as we see below, many try to offer as much support as they can, even when they find the prospect of a reunion quite threatening.

Finally, it is likely that many, perhaps most, adoptive parents will assume that their adopted son or daughter will be curious or might have already searched, but feel constrained from asking. In these circumstances it might be easier to reassure your parents by being open rather than having them fear the worst.

ADVICE BOX! ADVICE BOX! ADVICE BOX! ADVICE BOX! ADVICE BOX!

Pros and cons of telling adoptive family

Pros

- Having the support of the adoptive family is a precious gift, even if it is very tentative support at the beginning. Most people seem to need this emotional permission (although you cannot insist on it) and having it really does make a huge difference.

- Having told your adoptive family means that if the reunion does not work out then you will get more support from your adoptive family. This is not the same as having your cake and eating it – a reunion is not about trying to swap families. ▶

- Usually telling will eventually strengthen the relationship when adoptive parents find out that you are not going to disappear. Often, too, adopted people report that they appreciate their adoptive family more rather than less after a reunion.

- Living with a secret, and especially adoptive parents finding out about reunion by accident, is very difficult and stressful and can backfire badly.

Cons

- Most adoptive parents will feel anxious about their position after a reunion. Your relationship with them is likely be tested for a while and they may need lots of reassurance.

- Some adoptive parents will feel angry and betrayed by your decision to search. If this does happen try to understand their fears, be patient with them and try to give them as much reassurance as you can.

- Some adoptive parents will want to persuade you not to search as they fear you may get hurt or rejected. Often this reflects a genuine concern for your well-being, sometimes it might be based more on their own fears about losing you.

Only you can decide whether to tell or not to tell. You know your parents best. If telling is going to destroy your relationship with them, then you may need to think twice. Although, in most cases, telling can be difficult, it is usually the best option. However, there are no guarantees.

Having told

We have already mentioned that, in most cases, telling your adoptive parents works out reasonably well. We shall look at what happens over the longer term in the second half of the chapter but the majority of adoptive mothers and adoptive fathers are 'supportive' when first told about the search or reunion. However, in our findings, about one-third of adoptive parents were worried at the news and about 10 per cent reacted with anger. About a quarter of adopted people reported that they felt their relationship with their adoptive parents was put under strain initially, while around 60 per cent of people felt it remained unchanged at the beginning. A small number of adopted people said that the relationship actually improved.

Although the impact on your adoptive parents of telling is broadly positive, within this pattern there is much variation. Let us look in more detail, starting with the most positive responses.

Relaxed and supportive responses

Some adopted people find it very easy to talk to their adoptive parents about the search process. Making the decision to tell about the reunion is a relatively easy decision to make as the adoptive parents have always been free in sharing information about the adoption. They might even have signalled that they would be happy to support a search. Their reactions are relaxed and encouraging, with some parents going further, actually helping with the search process. This happened to Kenneth:

> **❝**They had always said if I ever wanted to find my mother they'd always help me. So I talked it over with them and said would you mind if I try and trace my mother? They said 'no, and we'll do everything to help you we can'. And they did. I mean they were always trying to help me. And I always said to them, when I do this I said 'you're always my mother and father and that will always remain, nothing will change'. I told them everything that went on, everything that happened, as it happened, all the way through. So I kept them fully informed of what was happening all the time. And they helped me all the time through it, so I mean they didn't miss out on any information, everything that happened as it happened, I told them. They were really very excited and they wanted to meet her as well. Brilliant. **❞**

When adoptive parents have always been open it is much easier to be open in return. In Kenneth's case, although his parents had already given their 'permission' for him to start a search he was also careful to get their permission explicitly before searching. He also reassured them of their continuing importance as parents. Not all adoptive parents want to help with the search or be kept fully informed of its progress, nor do all adopted people want to have them so closely involved. But it can be a good way of reassuring adoptive parents of their continuing significance.

Worried and hurt responses

A more common reaction, however, is for adoptive parents initially to feel a little hurt, worried or upset by the news of an impending search or reunion. It can sometimes bring to the surface old and deep feelings of not being the 'real' parent. They might be afraid that you will reject and replace them with your birth family. Indeed, most adopted people seem to assume that that is how their adoptive parents would feel. This sense of anxiety and hurt is graphically illustrated by Cora's account of her adoptive mother's reaction:

> **❝**My adoptive mother was just really hurt. She didn't want to be but she was. She felt threatened. She was worried, she told me later, that I'd meet my natural mother and get on with her like a house on fire and I would then have no use for and no desire to

be with my adoptive family. And her worry was rejection. And of course I completely understood that but there was a part of me that resented that, but I completely respected and understood it. **"**

The feelings of hurt and worry are entirely understandable. At the time of the adoption almost all adoptive parents would have been told to act as if they were the 'real' parents. Yet they might have felt some insecurity about their position, lacking that basic biological tie. These worries come to the surface, not surprisingly, with the prospect of the birth parent coming onto the scene. For many, it seems that the biological tie threatens to be more powerful than the many years of love, care and a shared history experienced with their adopted child. As we see later, however, in most cases this shared history is generally stronger than, or at least as strong as, any biological tie.

At the same time as feeling worried and threatened, many adoptive parents also feel that they have to do the 'right thing'. They try to encourage or support the search even if it feels as if they may lose their son or daughter. This was clearly true in David's case where his mother tried to put on a brave face despite her fears:

"I tested the water basically to see what their reaction would be. My dad couldn't be more supportive really. He said 'Yeah, we haven't got a problem with that, we've given you what we can in your childhood and obviously we'll be here to support you.' And my mum was very quiet but she said exactly the same. And I thought that it probably did upset her. And she said 'no, no, no, you carry on'. But it was her tone of voice and stuff. So in the end I mean she said 'you've got to do what you want to do, we're only here, I mean we've brought you up and you're an adult now, you're a man, and whoever she is she's not going to take you away from us and we'll always be here'. So I got it through. . . . **"**

David's case, like many others, highlights how complicated the responses of adoptive parents can be. Just as adopted people try to protect their parents as much as possible – clearly both Cora and David did as much as they could to reassure and soften the blow – so adoptive parents try to protect their children by not always revealing how upset they are.

It's also worth pointing out that your adoptive parents won't necessarily have the same response. Fathers, as in David's case, can be relatively relaxed while mothers might be very anxious. Or it might work the other way around with adoptive mothers being supportive and adoptive fathers feeling more threatened. Although we've focused on adoptive parents, some adoptive siblings also feel threatened by the prospect of a reunion, fearing that they too might be replaced by another birth sibling.

Anger and silencing

While some adoptive parents feel anxious yet supportive of their son's or daughter's search, a few parents feel angry, even betrayed. They might express their anger by refusing to acknowledge that the search or reunion is happening. Kim reported that:

"My adopted mother has been completely hopeless about the whole thing. 'I don't want to know about that bloody woman, why should I know about her, what's she ever done for you? Don't ever mention her name to me again'. And she has never asked about her, has never wanted to see a photo of her and assumes that because she's blotted it all out of her mind therefore I can't be seeing her again. As far as she's concerned it's a selfish thing – 'she gave you to me, she can't come back on the scene now'. We have such an appalling relationship anyway, it doesn't really matter."

We did not have any cases among our interviews of adoptive parents who were so angry that they broke off relations with their son or daughter. What did happen sometimes was an initial explosion of anger, and the adoptive parents refusing to hear any more about what was going on, as in Joanna's case:

"I told my father that I'd got the notes, that we had been to The Children's Society and found out about my actual adoption and he said then 'are you going to find out any more' and I said 'we haven't decided' which we hadn't, and he said 'well don't tell me if you do and don't ever mention any of this to your mother' . . ."

We should point out that while this degree of overt anger is fairly rare, it does happen. Even so, if you show your parents that you are not abandoning them, their anger may lessen in time.

Not telling

About 20 per cent of people in our research did not tell their adoptive parents about the search or reunion, or they delayed telling them long after reunion, or the adoptive parents found out later down the line. There are a number of reasons why people feel they can not tell or should put off telling, but the main one is a fear that their adoptive parents will be very hurt or feel rejected. In some cases, the desire not to tell also reflects worries about the strength of their relationship. Ava, for example, had kept her reunion secret for several years, partly to protect her parents but also because of a concern that she risked losing their love and support if they knew about the reunion:

"The reason I felt I couldn't tell them about it is because I just could not decipher what their reaction would be because it was never discussed. I just couldn't risk it. And you know what they say 'what you don't know, doesn't hurt you'. I plan to continue like that. I'm not going to hurt my mum and dad. I could explain until I'm blue in the face but I think if I was them I'd still think 'why does she feel it's necessary?' My dad especially – I will not take the risk to alienate my parents in any way whatsoever. It's too risky so I'm not going to ever tell them. I think the only thing negative about the whole thing is the guilt. I feel that I can't tell my mum and dad. And I really wish I could tell them because since leaving home my mum and dad have been such a great support in times when I've needed them. **"**

People who secretly go ahead with a reunion find themselves in a double bind. Ava felt guilty about not telling but also feared the consequences of telling. What might help in these situations is when adoptive parents are able to be more open and give some indication that they would support a search. However, even when this occurs, there are still those who are reluctant to tell their parents. This was Eleanor's position:

"I still feel uncomfortable when my mum tries to talk about anything 'close'. She did try and say a few times – 'if you ever want to trace I'll understand'. But I didn't want to talk about it. And then she said it again, and I thought 'here's my perfect opportunity to tell her' but I just couldn't bring myself to. And, of course, I'd left it so long as well, it was just getting harder and harder to tell them. I didn't want to hurt them, I feel as though I would really hurt them and they wouldn't understand why I had to do it. In actual fact it came out when my brother did trace, and he decided to tell my mum all along. Mum was talking to me about my brother and what he'd done and I said 'oh actually . . . I have traced as well', and she said 'I thought you might have' and I said 'well actually I've met them as well'. She took it really well. She's just really glad I told her but she's hurt that I took so long. But if you can tell them at the time – certainly not leaving it seven or eight years! **"**

There is no easy solution to the problem of telling or not telling, not least because many adoptive parents and adoptive people feel that the prospect of a reunion might threaten their relationship. However, and in the long run, it is probably wiser to be open, to tell, and look for support.

ADVICE BOX! ADVICE BOX! ADVICE BOX! ADVICE BOX! ADVICE BOX!

Making the decision to tell

It is often difficult to predict exactly how parents will react to the possibility of search and reunion. Even if you haven't talked about adoption or searching it does not mean that your parents have not been thinking about it. Do not forget that almost all parents know that searching and reunion is now possible – and they are likely to have wondered about whether you will do it, or have done it.

You might get some clues or pointers about their possible reaction from:

- Messages about adoption and searching – how open were your parents during your childhood and more recently about adoption or searching?

- How do your parents react if the topic comes up on TV, in the papers or in conversation?

- Have any of your brothers or sisters searched? How did your parents react?

- What is your relationship like with your adoptive parents? How easy is it to talk about sensitive topics?

And some ideas for raising the topic:

- Search and reunion frequently appear in the media with stories about real-life reunions or fictional plots in soaps and films. This can be a good starting point to start a conversation.

- You could raise the issue as a 'what if?' – for example, mentioning that you have been thinking about searching and asking your parents how they would feel if you did go ahead.

It's also worth thinking about:

- Ideally what would you like to happen?

- If you could put yourself in their shoes, what do you think you would like to happen?

Making life easier for everyone

To an extent, when adoptive parents have been relatively open about the adoption, it is much easier both to predict their reaction and to tell them about a search. However, even if there have been uncomfortable silences about adoption, it does not necessarily mean that telling parents about search and reunion will backfire or undermine the relationship. We found that the majority of adopted people said they had felt uncomfortable talking about adoption, but in the end most were able to inform their parents about the search and this generally worked out well. Such openness is not always easy, however, and can sometimes test the relationship.

It will probably help if you strike a balance between being sensitive to your parents' feelings and being true to your own needs. Not many adoptive parents welcome the prospect of a reunion with open arms. Those who feel hurt or angry can sometimes behave 'unreasonably'. This is hard to accept when you most want their support. It may well help to try to make sense of why they react in such a manner. In most cases the hurt and anger is about their fear of losing you to another. The prospect of reunion raises the possibility of rejection, for you, for them, for your family. The biggest fear of adopted people is that they will be rejected by a birth relative, but adoptive parents also fear that they themselves will be rejected and replaced. As a result, your parents may say some hurtful things or possibly become a bit distant. Probably the best way of dealing with this is to put yourself in their shoes, think about why they might be behaving in that way, and give them as much reassurance as you can, as Una illustrates:

> **❝**Finding my natural father has changed my relationship with my parents. It's also tested them because they believed that I was going to just forget them completely and I had to prove to them that I wasn't that type of person and I did appreciate everything they'd done for me. I just tried to put myself into their shoes and understand their fear. So I did get to know them a lot better, almost as if I suddenly saw them as human beings more than I had done when I was living with them. And I could see that they were really really scared, so I had to really respect that. **❞**

Part of being sensitive is to allow your parents to move forward at their own pace. In many cases the passage of time, and the fact that the adopted person does not abandon the adoptive family, eases the tension and allays the fears of adoptive parents. Some parents want to get as much information about the reunion as soon as possible, but others make it clear that they want to take things much more slowly, again quoting Una:

> **❝**My adoptive mother's been able to take on board just little snippets of information at different stages. So she knew that I'd found my father initially and I left it at that. And then she asked me 'were there any brothers and sisters?' So I gave her that. It was almost like I was just answering the questions that she asked – because she felt able to cope with that bit of information at that time. Now she's met my sister. So when I talk to my Mum she always asks about my sister and she writes to her. She hasn't met my Dad. But I know my Mum will tell me if she's ready to do that and I'll leave it till then. **❞**

Irrespective of how important it is to be thoughtful, fair and sensitive towards your adoptive parents, it is just as important that you remain true to yourself and your own needs. You have a moral as well as a legal right to search for a birth relative if that is what you want. Nevertheless, the watchwords of *sensitivity*, *support* and *openness* remain, and given the intensity and complexity of emotions involved there are bound to be some problems. Having someone to talk to who is not directly involved may well help you to untangle some of your own feelings and think about strategies for making things easier. Your adoptive parents might appreciate having someone to talk to as they are directly affected by the search and reunion and might feel that they have very little control over developments. Most adoption agencies will offer support to adoptive parents. Talking to a counsellor might not offer a complete solution, but it can give back some feeling of control, as Wendy reports:

> **❝**They spoke to the counsellor and they did take some advice and they actually had a counsellor come and see them – which I think helped – mum said it certainly clarified a few points and she said it did prepare them for what to expect over the next few months and years. And when I spoke to her last she said 'well you know she's been right all the way through'. **❞**

Above all try not to panic if everything is not smooth and plain sailing at the beginning. In practice the ties between adopted people and their parents are strong, very few relationships break down and quite a few emerge stronger as a result of having faced the challenge posed by the reunion. We shall look at this in more detail in the next section.

Ideas for situations where adoptive parents are angry or very anxious about reunion

- Parents can feel hurt or angry. In most cases they are not just being unreasonable but are hurt or angry because they feel threatened.

- Give them time. As the reunion progresses they will find that they will not be replaced.

- Reassure them in words and actions.

- Encourage them to talk to a counsellor, or someone who has been through the experience or a sibling or other family member who can help them to talk through their feelings.

- You may well feel angry if your parents are not giving you support or encouragement. It is probably best to try to work through your anger by talking with someone else rather than risking a confrontation with them.

- Try to keep some form of communication open, even if it is difficult. If you withdraw from them it will only confirm their worst fears.

- Try to go at their pace in giving information. If you can try to give them a realistic picture of how the reunion is going – the things that are going well and things that are not so easy. Their worst fear might be that you are in a wonderful reunion with a 'perfect' birth parent who will replace them. A realistic picture will shatter that fantasy without giving the false impression that you have made a mistake by having a reunion.

- If you are an adoptive parent, and if you feel anxious or worried, then say so – it will give your son or daughter the chance to reassure you. Try to work out why you feel like you do. Can you put yourself in the shoes of the adopted person and think about why they might be curious about their origins? Do not forget that in the majority of cases the relationship with the adoptive family is unchanged or comes out stronger after a reunion, especially if you can offer some support to it.

Balancing families

We've been looking at the initial reactions of adoptive parents to the news of search and reunion. In this section we fast forward to see the longer-term impact of the reunion on the relationship with the adoptive parents as well as how people manage to relate to both their adoptive and birth families. We shall begin with some statistics and then look in more depth at the various ways adopted people handle having two families.

A key finding from our research is that reunions seldom do much harm to the relationship between adopted people and their parents, and in many cases the relationship is strengthened. Over half of adopted people said that their appreciation of their adoptive family increased post-reunion. That is not to say that it will be plain sailing all the time. Most adoptive parents need a lot of reassurance that they are not going to be replaced. In some cases, this tests the relationship. But as Val and Zara discovered, in the end, bonds can be strengthened:

> ❝I feel as though sometimes I've betrayed my parents by actually taking the path to find out more about my natural parents. I know at times it's given them quite a lot of pain. But although there's been upset and traumas, I think it's really positive for everybody – even my parents and my brother. Because through talking over the years they've realised that perhaps they can see me in a new light and think 'yes, she really really does love us'. Because this was a test and they've come through it.❞
>
> Val

> ❝It was upsetting for them, and their hearts were telling them one thing and their minds were telling them another. They thought they were going to lose me after all these years – they didn't know what was going to happen, it was the unexpected. My Mum was like 'oh you are going to love this Mum that's really trendy and wears hipsters still!' And in the end they have come round to it. And my life hasn't changed a great deal and my relationship with them hasn't changed a great deal – if not got stronger.❞
>
> Zara

A second important finding is that the relationship with the adoptive family tends to remain strong and more active than with the birth family. The blood tie is significant, and we have already seen that reunions with birth family members generally last. But it also seems that growing up in a family and having a shared history is important too, perhaps even more important than the blood tie:

- Five years or more after the initial reunion 67 per cent of searchers were in regular weekly contact with their adoptive mothers compared to 24 per cent in weekly contact with their birth mothers.
- Sixty per cent of adopted people felt more 'at home' in their adoptive family.

However, while for most people the tie with the adoptive family is stronger, there are different ways in which the balance between the adoptive and birth families is struck. Just over half of the people in our study said they related mainly or exclusively to their adoptive mothers eight years after the reunion. Twenty per cent said they had an equally good relationship with both of their mothers. However, 13 per cent reported that they now related mainly to their birth mother, and in a very few cases were no longer in regular contact with their adoptive parents.

We shall now look in a little more detail at the different ways in which adopted people manage their relationships with two families at once and the strength of contact, if any, there is between the two.

The family expanders

These are reunions where the adopted person has warm and positive relationships with the birth mother (and her family) as well as with the adoptive family. The adoptive parents support the reunion. All relationships seem relaxed and inclusive from the outset, with no sense of competition or conflict between birth and adoptive parents. The definition of 'family' is expanded by the reunion, bringing in the birth mother and her family, with both mothers given roughly 'equal' status. Both birth and adoptive parents are relaxed about each other and acknowledge and support their respective relationships with their son or daughter. Dawn, for example, describes her delight at how her reunion had worked out:

> "They talk to each other, my adoptive Mum says 'how's your Mum and Dad'. My biological Mum phones me – she'll say 'say hello to your Mum and Dad for me' – and they've met each other and . . . Mum and Dad came down and they come round to meet Mum – then they met each other again at the wedding. I've always dreamt of that – that one day I'll get married and they'd be there – and they were – it was brilliant."

Harry describes a similar situation where the lack of competition between parents meant that he was not forced to choose or to take sides:

> "They actually spoke on the phone, the two mums. And that was quite emotional for both I think. Mum was sort of thanking her for me and she was thanking Mum for looking after me and bringing me up and all the rest of it. And then the first Christmas after that my adoptive mum did a photo album, a selection of photographs, from as a baby right the way through to an adult and she gave it to her as a Christmas present. She had no photographs of me, so then she had photographs right the way through."

This type of reunion can work out extremely well. Both sets of parents are able to feel included and the adopted person does not have to face any conflicts of loyalty. This relatively happy state is not easy to achieve. It does require having two sets of parents who feel secure enough in their relationship with you to welcome the other. Not all parents, either adoptive parents or birth parents feel comfortable coming together in this way – nor will all adopted people want this type of reunion.

Realistically resigned

In some cases, adopted people want the chance to bring their birth and adoptive families together, but this does not seem possible. In 'realistically resigned' reunions, the adopted person has a successful reunion with a birth relative but at least one of the adoptive parents finds the reunion threatening. In these cases, adopted people reach a point where they accept that not all relationships are going to be harmonious or ideal. They are disappointed, sometimes angry, about the position taken by their adoptive parents, but they understand it. Although they would have liked both sets of parents to meet and to be comfortable together, they remain realistic enough to accept that it probably is not going to happen or have a future beyond a one-off meeting. In her reflections, Wendy says:

> ❝My parents are generally pretty easy-going, but my mum winds herself up like a top and in fact when she last met my birth mother in June she made herself ill. She said 'how stupid can you get? Every time I look at her I think you're only human, you are not a big monster'. Actually if we put them all together in a room they get on fine. But I don't think it would be a good idea to try to make them be friends. They've only got one thing in common at the end of the day and that's me. They've got their own lives and I think it's best to leave it.❞

Similarly, Val felt like she had to tread on eggshells, wanting to include her adoptive parents in the reunion but recognising that they did not really want to be included:

> ❝My mother saw my natural mother as a threat. And many a time we thought about trying to get everybody to meet but my mum just doesn't feel that she'd ever be able to do that. But gradually over time things have got better and now I'm able to say 'oh I spent the evening with her' without my mum just slamming the phone down or bursting into tears. I think I'm realistic to realise that they are never going to be best chums or anything – maybe one day they'll cross paths – but I don't think there will ever be a really positive relationship there. Just more of an acceptance I think.❞

If you had hoped to bring together the two parts of your life, then it can be deeply frustrating if one side is hostile or reluctant. The reality, however, is that bringing people together who are not going to get on or do not want to meet is likely to be counterproductive. Things may change over time, but if they do not you will have to accept matters and keep the two relationships separate.

Separate worlds

In actual fact not all adopted people want to bring both adoptive and birth families together, whether or not it is possible. For some it feels much more comfortable to keep the two families apart, with the adopted person having separate relationships with each family and firm boundaries between them. Sometimes, in these 'separate worlds' reunions, there is a sense in which the firm boundaries are a way of protecting the adoptive mother as well as the adopted person from an emotional and committed birth mother, as David says:

> **"**My birth mother would want to see me every day of the week, to make up for lost time I suppose, but I'm saying 'no that's not possible'. I'm keeping this life here and when I'm with her I'll be her son but when I'm here that's my mum and dad. I've got two separate lives really. I try and keep both happy really. My father was very open and wanted to meet her. But my mum was very quiet. She didn't say 'no I don't want to do it', but she didn't say 'yes I do want to do it'. I don't think she really did want to do it so I never have done.**"**

Nicola's approach was very similar, keeping her two families separate at least in part to protect her adoptive mother:

> **"**My birth mother says that she would like to meet my parents and my mum said she wouldn't mind if that's what I want. She would do it but she doesn't know how to cope with that. With Mary, she said that she would like to meet my mum and dad but that's not going to happen because I don't want that either. I don't want to put my mum and dad in a position where they meet Mary. I know my mum and she would be on the defensive all the time.**"**

'Closed ranks' reunions

So far we have looked at reunions where strong relationships are maintained with both the adoptive and birth families. However, as we have already seen, this balance is not always possible and the relationship with one of the families is shaky or non-existent. More commonly, it is the relationship with the birth family, or more specifically the birth mother, that does not develop. Where the relationship with the birth mother remains difficult, especially in the 'push–pull' or testing state (see Chapter 4), some adopted people develop much stronger relationships with their adoptive families than they had had previously, largely at the expense of building the relationship with the birth family, as in Joanna's case:

> **"**So has it affected your relationship with your adopted parents – although they don't know about it? I think it's made me closer. But I value them more. I know it sounds unkind but it's almost like they rescued me from the life that I don't think I could have accepted.**"**

These 'closed ranks' reunions do maintain a relationship with the birth family, but it is more difficult and less active than the relationship with the adoptive family. There is another 'closed ranks' group in which the relationship with the birth family never develops. These are situations where a birth relative makes contact with the adopted person via an intermediary service but where the approach is deeply unwelcome (see also Chapter 8). These are adopted people who identify strongly with their adoptive family and feel that the approach is an invasion of their family life. In these cases very little if any contact is established and, if anything, the perceived threat leads the adopted person to move even closer to the adoptive family. Charlotte, for example, describes a meeting of her adoptive family where they collectively decided on a strategy, leading eventually to a single unsatisfactory meeting with her birth mother:

> ❝We went on talking for hours my parents, my brother and me. And it came up again, in bits, over the weekend – and they said 'go ahead with it if that's what you want to do'. It was decided that we would write. We talked about it a lot. And we actually improved our relationship in some way – although I would say it was a very good relationship anyway. ❞

'Transferrers' and 'adrift' reunions

So far the different patterns we have identified have been based on an ongoing relationship with the adoptive family after reunion – sometimes very positive, sometimes a little strained, sometimes protective. In a few cases the relationship with the adoptive family becomes very strained or breaks down. In 'transferrer' reunions, the relationship with the adoptive family breaks down after a new relationship is established with the birth family, while in 'adrift' reunions the reunion is followed by a collapse of the relationship with both adoptive and birth families. Both patterns are rare.

Ian's reunion was one of the few examples of a 'transferrer' relationship. He had had a long and very close reunion with his birth parents (who had subsequently married after the adoption) but when his adoptive parents were eventually told, they were very angry. The relationship had not completely broken down but was much less active than that with the birth parents:

> ❝It's caused a lot of friction I think, getting to know my biological parents, between myself and my mother and father who adopted me. They seem to have put up barriers to us meeting as regularly. They are always quite busy and if I want to see them I've basically got to make an appointment, which kind of makes it worse, because with Jean and Charlie I can just turn up. I think they're angry. They're not happy about it and for reasons that I find hard to establish. But in a way they created this situation themselves in the beginning by adopting me, they've done the running on that side of it, so they have to accept the consequences as much as I do and they've really got to get used to it, I can't change the way I am, and I can't change the circumstances. ❞

Although Ian's relationship with his adoptive family was difficult, he did have a very strong relationship with his birth family. In some 'adrift' cases the relationship with both families is fragile. Rochelle, for example, had had a very fraught relationship with her adoptive parents before the reunion. The reunion did not work out well and she was left with very weak family ties or support:

> ❝I don't have much contact with my [adoptive] family, because their love, for want of a better word, doesn't do anything for me practically, never does anything for me,

it doesn't give me good feelings, it's not supportive, it's not ever there. I really put my pride on the line to discuss this with them because I really felt it was nothing to do with them – I did not need them to be involved. But no one was really interested in it. . . . And in fact I think that the relationship within my birth father's family is, was, pretty similar to my own adopted family and I couldn't believe I've got two of them. And my birth mother's family's pretty fucked up actually! And when I turned up I think it reawakened unresolved feelings that she hadn't, things that she had not dealt with. And I felt that I had to do all I could, having opened this hornet's nest, to be supportive, but I ended up feeling smothering by her, it ended up being a really difficult relationship where I felt I had to tread carefully around and cater to her needs and sensitivities at the expense of mine.**"**

Not many people have to face a situation where relationships with both adoptive and birth families do not work out. If this situation does occur, it is still important to keep some form of communication open with one or other family. You might find more common ground at a later time. In the meantime, make sure that you get as much support as you can to help you to deal with the situation.

Summary

- Most adopted people face a difficult choice about whether to tell their adoptive parents about a search or reunion and face hurting them, or to go behind their backs and live a secret life. It can be a hard choice but most people do tell. The most common response from parents is an attempt to be as supportive as possible even if they do feel worried or anxious about what the search and reunion will mean for themselves and for the adopted person.

- The initial 'telling' phase is usually the hardest part. In the long run most people's relationship with their adoptive parents remains unchanged, or actually gets better as the relationship comes through the test posed by the search.

- It is more common for people to end up closer to their adoptive parents than their birth parents, but there is a lot of variation.

- There are all sorts of different ways in which people relate to their two families. Some people want to bring families together; others want this to happen but can't bring it about; and yet others are happy to keep both parents and their families separate. Some people relate much more strongly to their adoptive family, others to their birth family. Sometimes relationships with both families break down.

- The search and reunion process is tough for most adoptive parents. They can feel very threatened by birth relatives coming onto the scene. Most will try to do the right thing and try to support the reunion even though they feel anxious. Some will be very angry or will withdraw from you. Ideally they should offer you support as you set out on the reunion trail, but sometimes their fears mean that this is just not going to happen. All you can do is to be as patient as you can, and give them as much reassurance as you can.

Rejection and reunions that break down

The material presented in this chapter provides some ideas that might enable adopted people to make sense of a rejection or a reunion that breaks down.

Introduction

At some point almost everyone with some connection with adoption and adoption reunion will have felt or feared rejection. Of course all relationships – friendships, partnerships, even work relationships – can make people vulnerable to feelings of rejection, but there is something very powerful about adoption and reunion that seems to make the issue particularly salient. At some level, many adopted people feel a sense of rejection from when they were originally placed for adoption by their birth mother. Many birth mothers, in turn, worry that the adopted person will feel rejected. If you are at the stage of thinking about having a reunion you may well be worried that your birth relatives will not want to know you, or that your approach might simply be ignored, or that after you have met the other person may decide not to see you again. Sometimes a fear of rejection can stop you going through with a search even though you would like to meet a birth relative.

On the other side of the fence, some birth relatives can also be afraid to search because they fear a rejection or may indeed already have had their approach turned down. In the chapters on reunions with birth mothers and birth fathers we looked at how a fear of rejection can impact on how relationships develop. And as we have just seen in Chapter 7, rejection is also a significant issue for adoptive parents who worry about being replaced by the birth family.

Our focus in this chapter is on those reunions that never get established, where one party rejects contact or where the reunion breaks down immediately. We look at both types of rejection, emphasising, however, that neither is common. We then explore some of the reasons why rejection occurs, looking as far as possible, from the perspective of both adopted people and birth relatives who refuse or break off contact. Our aim in presenting this material is to provide some ideas that might enable people who are on the receiving end of a rejection to make sense of it. The second half of the chapter looks at how people react to rejection and gives some ideas about how to come to terms with what is inevitably a very painful experience.

The likelihood of initial rejection or rejection after contact

The first thing that we should say is that rejection does not happen very often. The great majority of birth relatives who are approached by an adopted person want to have contact. Similarly, most adopted people approached by an intermediary on behalf of a birth relative go on to have a reunion. It is only in a minority of cases that the person approached refuses to exchange information or have a meeting. In our research, only 7 per cent of adopted people trying to make contact with a birth relative (mostly birth mothers) were rejected outright, that is 19 out of 274 searchers. The picture was similar for birth relative-initiated contacts. Only 10 per cent of adopted people refused to have contact with a birth relative. Overall then, less than 10 per cent of reunions, initiated by *either* a birth relative *or* an adopted person, result in an initial rejection.

There are also some reunions that cease after one or two letters or face-to-face meetings. This happened in 7 per cent of reunions with birth mothers, 10 per cent of reunions with birth fathers, and 12 per cent of reunions with birth siblings. A small number of birth relative-initiated reunions also ended after a first meeting.

Apparent reasons for rejections and early endings

The message from our research is that an outright rejection or ending the contact after a single meeting is fairly rare. This should reassure you if you are contemplating a contact with a birth relative. At the same time, however, these reassurances offer little comfort to those who have been rejected or have had a contact ended after only one two exchanges. If you are in this situation, the obvious question for you is: If rejection is relatively rare, why has it happened to me? Let us look at some of the reasons why rejection or early closure happens.

Initial rejection: clear messages

One of the great difficulties for those who experience an immediate rejection is trying to understand exactly why it happened. In some cases, the person making the approach gets a message that the person being contacted does not want an approach or does not wish to respond. In other cases, there is simply a resounding silence. We shall look first at those situations where the contacted person, either a birth relative or adopted person, does respond, albeit negatively.

When the rejection is clear and unambiguous, it tends to draw on two, often related, reasons – a lack of feelings for, or interest in, the other person, or a sense that the other person represents a threat to the contacted person's world.

Being told that a birth parent, perhaps especially a birth mother, admits no feelings for you is very difficult and hard for most people to understand. Here is how Gemma describes her birth mother's 'callous' response to an approach via an intermediary:

❝She wrote back and said she didn't want anything to do with it. I was hurt, very hurt as she didn't want to know. Very hurt now that she still doesn't want to know. I thought that she might change her mind, but she said she gave me up when she was 18 and she's got a new life now. And the other part was she said she had no love for me, and from when I was born until I was adopted my grandparents looked after me, so she said she had no feelings for me. We're still getting no response. I've written recently a few letters which I've got back. I'm still hurt now that she's still rejecting me and I'm cross that she won't even meet me, just a meeting so we can talk. That's all I want is to meet her and have a chat, to find out why I got adopted and a bit about my past. But all she does is write back in letters – 'I've told you what's happened, I don't want to meet you, I've got no feelings, if I see you it would be no feelings.' She writes as Dear Miss Smith, not Dear Gemma, and she always signs it Mrs Adams, she doesn't write it Mary. And the way she writes is callous and she's got no feeling.**❞**

Similar sentiments are expressed in the following two letters written by a birth mother to her daughter and an intermediary. The birth mother had written saying that she did not want contact as she had never had any maternal feelings towards her daughter. She said she was also worried about the impact a reunion would have on her own life.

Box 1. **Letter written to the adopted person**

Dear Annie,

This is the first time I have written to you and it is also my last. Thank you for your letter, I will answer your questions if I can.

I will begin by telling you about your father, he was a charmer, until I fell pregnant, that is! . . . He soon ditched me and left me to sort myself out on my own. . . . I must admit that I hadn't planned a child and I have no maternal instincts whatsoever, in fact I have never liked babies and I still don't. There was no question as to my next move and I did this without telling anyone at all. I left home and got on with it. Not every woman is meant to become a mother you know and I knew it wasn't for me. I hated being pregnant and I was sick for 7 of the 9 months which didn't help. I never heard from your father again and I wouldn't want to anyway.

I do hope that all is well with you and your adoptive parents, as they are your real parents who brought you up and cared for you and did everything for you. I have done none of these things and am just a name to you.

Box 2.	Letter written to the counsellor

Dear Madam,

I just don't have any feelings towards her. I didn't cry at the time and haven't wished anything different at any time since. If at the time I had feelings for the father perhaps things would have been different. . . . Looking back I should have been advised to terminate. Why I didn't have her adopted at an early stage I don't know because I never loved her. If I did I could not have given her up later and not cared. I know this is hard but that is how it is. I had no feelings, which I still don't have. I never loved her, which you can't just start doing now.

As you are on her side, please tell her to leave me alone. No good will come. Only hurt for her. No happy families which she would like. I don't want to live my life thinking who is on the phone, at the door or what comes in the post. I have my rights to my privacy and I have made enquiries and there are things I can do and I will to protect my own family.

I have no intention of making contact or sending photos and I have no interest in having any back. I have no interest in her at all. I don't care what happens in her life, in the future or in the past.

Letters such as these or messages sent via an intermediary that a birth parent has no feelings for or interest in you are likely to be shattering. It is hard for any of us to see the person as anything other than callous or unnatural. But it might also be worth remembering that for many birth mothers the circumstances of the adoption may have been traumatic and she may have had no one to support her. One way of dealing with this is to try to wipe out or suppress any feelings for the child who was given away.[1] An approach by an adopted person many years later may be seen as a real threat to the way in which the birth mother has tried to deal with the situation. She buried her feelings and fears their resurrection.

In some cases, the sense of threat might also be as a result of having long hidden the fact of the adoption from family, friends and neighbours. In the past it was common for unmarried mothers to be sent away to have the baby in secret and then be told to forget about the child. A birth mother or father may subsequently feel unable to have contact if she or he has not told anyone about the adoption. This absolute dread of long-concealed secrets being revealed appears very strongly in Lawrence's account of his birth mother's response to his approach:

---

[1] A useful book to read on the experience of birth mothers is *Half a Million Women: Mothers Who Lose Their Children By Adoption* by David Howe, Phillida Sawbridge and Diana Hinings, first published in 1992 by Penguin, now available through The Post-Adoption Centre, Torriano Mews, London.

> ❝She phoned the intermediary and said she couldn't meet me. In a very frightened tone saying 'no one knows, no one knows at all about this. It's been a secret with me all these years.' And she sent a letter with really shaky handwriting. It's just a scrap of paper, no address at all, two or three sentences. It says here: 'Please can you pass this on to Lawrence. I beg you to let this be the end; it would be the finish of me if it went any further. Please I beg of you.' Very final. And there was a letter to me inside and a couple of photographs. It says 'because it was a shock to hear about you, I hope you don't mind but I would rather not hear anymore, please please – underlined twice – my family do not know about you, it would wreck my life if they did. I am enclosing a couple of snaps, please please can you let this be the end of the matter, I beg of you. I'm sorry.' ❞

Lawrence's birth mother's reaction is perhaps a little easier to understand than those who disavow any feeling. Certainly Lawrence's reaction was one of sympathy for her plight, but nevertheless it was still a difficult experience with which to come to terms:

> ❝And I didn't feel it was rejection, I just felt that she was so frightened. She'd kept this secret for all these years, and she couldn't tell anyone and it was very hard for her. But speaking to my mother-in-law, she can't understand it. She's of the same age. She cannot understand how you can give a child up. I couldn't have done that, she says, I couldn't have done that. So then you think, it's not rejection but you think, if she hadn't or if she'd been able to meet me and talk. ❞

So far we have only looked at birth mothers as those who are doing the rejecting. However, some of the same issues also come across in the reasons why *adopted people* reject an approach to them from a birth relative. We've looked in earlier chapters at how many adopted people felt a strong sense of connection with their birth families. But this was not true of all adopted people. Some adopted people, like some birth relatives, also said they did not feel any interest in or connection with their birth relatives and identified with their adoptive family alone (see also Chapter 9). As Stuart says:

> ❝I don't consider myself as adopted as such. It doesn't occur to me. I don't walk around every time I see my parents, I don't say, 'Oh hi, they're my adopted parents'. They are my parents. Period, that's it. It's only when something reminds me that I'm adopted that I realise. So otherwise the normal state of affairs is I consider them as my natural parents. ❞

And similarly, Charlotte:

> ❝I've never felt this need to understand and know about my 'roots' – which is gone on about so much in the papers all the time now. ❞

For this group, then, the prospect of a reunion was not seen as an opportunity, but very much as a threat to their sense of self and to their family, much like the response of some birth mothers. Graham was contacted by an intermediary on behalf of his sister and found it deeply upsetting and unsettling and chose not to have any contact:

> **"**This letter came through [from the intermediary]. I was in a real state. I was in floods of tears in the office. They've changed me forever. They [the adoption society] set me up with a wonderful life and now they are trying to knock it down again. I don't have that feeling for a potential sister that will put them suddenly number one in the queue. They cannot become as important as my family and friends. I've got my family. I don't need another one.**"**

As with the birth mothers, many people will find it hard to believe or understand that someone can really be not interested in their background. It may be that, for some adopted people, having to put up such a strong defence is based on a real fear of the unknown or of a rejection in turn, or it may just simply be how they feel. Nonetheless, these feelings must be respected.

Initial rejection: unclear messages

Not all those who experience an immediate rejection actually get a response from the contacted person. Not getting any response to an approach is incredibly frustrating and difficult to deal with, not least because it makes it much harder to come to terms with why it has occurred. As one interviewee commented: 'I feel a complete rejection would be easier to cope with than being ignored!'

We can only speculate about why some people make no response. It may be for the reasons noted above, about not having any feelings, or experiencing a sense of threat. In some cases, there may be more specific factors. One situation where there seem to be a slightly higher number of rejections is where the birth mother and birth father had actually married after the adoption (although we should point out that many approaches to these parents also work out extremely well). In these cases, the adopted people had expected that their birth parents would be more willing to have contact. The refusal might be caused by the guilt and shame some parents feel at the prospect of telling their other children about the relinquishment of their first child, and old reminders of the stress experienced when the decision was made to 'give up' their child for adoption.

Rejection after contact

We described in Chapter 4 the wide variation in reactions to the first meeting. Most people reported positive feelings about the person being met. But about 20 per cent of searchers felt confused, while another 15 per cent felt distant, or that the other person was like a stranger. Not all of these reunions broke down, but in a small number of cases there were no further meetings.

A range of reasons exist for these relationships not moving on. In some cases it is due to a perception that the birth relative is too different, or perhaps has too many personal problems. A decision is then made not to take the relationship any further. This was the case with Charlotte, one of our interviewees, who had a single meeting initiated by her birth mother. But Charlotte felt uncomfortable and found her birth mother odd. Fraser, similarly had a single meeting with a half-sibling but formed an instant negative impression and decided against further contact:

> **❝**I arrived and I knocked on the door and he opened the door and, bearing in mind that that was the first time I'd seen him in person, that was the moment I rejected. I think it's true to say I'd gone there with trepidation, not really certain what I was doing. It had to be done but in a strange way I wished it didn't, but it had to. And when he opened the door, I didn't actually take to him as a person and he also had a black eye and I had an instant feeling that things were not right for a ready-made new family for me. And I think it was that moment in time that I'd gone a bridge too far and I realised that I'd probably have been better off keeping it at research level only and calling it a day. I spent three and a half hours there. I withdrew as tactfully as I possibly could without saying anything. I eventually plucked up enough courage to phone him and tell him that I couldn't actually see a future in our relationship. He did write a letter to me which was not particularly pleasant saying that he was upset by it, that he didn't really want to take me over particularly and that he felt very badly . . . done by . . . and that he would not contact me any more. I had nothing against them as such, it was that I personally had rejected that relationship on the door, I did not identify with him.**❞**

All reunions involve taking a leap into the unknown, with no guarantee that the person you will meet will be someone that you will like, get on with, or share similar lifestyles. The stories by Fraser and Charlotte highlight the need to be fully committed to take that step. In both cases they felt rather reluctant. It is very easy to get caught up in the process of reunion and move onto the next stage without being fully ready, in case either you are rejected or you are the one who does not want to take things further. Give yourself all the time you need before you move on.

Reunions can have a more fragmented or blurry ending, almost petering out without having ever really been established. Two of our interviewees, Kezia and Eleanor, both had some initial contact that did not go any further. Kezia is a person of mixed ethnicity with a white birth mother. Kezia had written to her birth mother and received a reply, but there was no subsequent contact. Here is her story:

> **❝**How do you write? Hello, this is me. Umm, I had a huge problem with that. It took several drafts to actually produce something and then she wrote back to me. She said she had expected it and had thought about me and she was pleased that I had got on and done so well, whatever. But it wasn't a case of, 'please contact me, it would be nice to see how you are doing or who you are'. Nothing at all like that. I know that she said we will exchange letters first of all, a couple of letters and then the possibility of meeting. The plan was to exchange letters for a while. I was very disappointed in the response and I thought, okay, I'll just drop it and that was it. I've got my photograph. I saw it as something coming to an end. It was just a black thing, it was just a big racial

thing and that was it. I thought I'm not going to try and promote myself as a black person. I felt that it's difficult when you know that it's a racial issue and there's a block there anyway. I didn't want it to affect me too much. I didn't want to get into this like eating myself up about it and sort of thinking oh, she doesn't want to know or all this kind of rejection stuff again. I really didn't want to go there and that's probably why I stopped abruptly like that. I mean Christ, who is she? She's not anybody really and I mean that sounds quite nasty in a way but she's not anybody and nor is my biological father, they're not anybody really. **"**

Eleanor's reunion with both her birth mother and birth father also petered out after one or two meetings. The third meeting with her birth mother was cancelled and no further letter contact developed:

"I think I actually said once in a letter 'if you don't want to keep in touch fine, I'll understand, but if you could just write and explain why it would make it easier' which she never did. And now I can't remember if I actually imagined writing that. I suppose fundamentally I didn't want to upset the apple-cart because I knew she hadn't told the rest of the family and she didn't want to tell them. **"**

It was a similar pattern with her birth father:

"He wrote a letter after we met, saying how much he'd enjoyed meeting me and then he said 'if you want to, we'd love to meet you again or keep in touch' and I sent him a card from holiday and stuff and about two years later I rang because I was in the area and then the phone was just put down and that's the last contact I've ever had with him either. I suppose I do feel a loss in so far as I've contacted them and now I've lost them again. I probably don't really acknowledge the rejection because there's question marks in both cases. I can take it whatever way I want to, depending on the mood I'm in really. Both left it slightly open-ended. Maybe if there's any contact in the future it's got to come via somebody else not me, so that I can get some concrete answer. But if it's got to be me. I don't want to lay myself open for that to happen to me. **"**

In both Eleanor's and Kezia's cases we do not know how their birth relatives felt about the reunion. Reading between the lines it would appear that the birth parents were relatively open to the prospect of further meetings but probably came across as cautious rather than enthusiastic. Making the first move in the reunion takes tremendous courage. But then asking for further meetings also forces you to put yourself on the line, with the possibility of facing a further rejection. In some way it probably requires even more courage as the request has become more personal. You are no longer unknown and the other person is reacting having already communicated with you or met you. This requires a lot of self-confidence, particularly if, as with Eleanor and Kezia, the other person is also anxious or cautious. Asking for further meetings also means that you need to feel entitled to claim a relationship or a place in the family. If you do not feel this right, and the relationship is not being offered enthusiastically, there is a chance that you might withdraw or retreat too soon in order to protect yourself from a rejection that is not necessarily going to happen.

This uncertainty about whether or not the relationship continues may be much less if you are welcomed with open arms. But some birth relatives are as anxious about rejection as you. Or they might be concerned about what the reunion might mean for them and their present families. In these situations both sides need to proceed cautiously as well as signal that they do want things to develop. This highlights the need to embark on the reunion only when you are as prepared as you can possibly be, when you feel strong, and when you have really good support. For some adopted people, the temptation might be to seek a reunion as a way of making them feel better about things. If you have had a difficult adoption or have personal problems then it is important to look after yourself in the best way possible. Give yourself time to work through some of these issues, maybe with a counsellor, before setting out on the reunion process that can be a challenging business at the best of times.

Reactions to rejection

Initial reactions

Not surprisingly, those who do experience a rejection find it very hard to accept. The immediate feelings are mainly ones of frustration, hurt, upset and anger. For those who are rejected immediately, it is difficult to understand why your birth relative does not feel as curious as you do. As Claire said:

> ❝I could acknowledge that it was difficult for her [birth mother], that she had two other children, that maybe her husband made it difficult as well. I could acknowledge that she probably had a really hard time of it because I assume that she went back to her parents and carried on her life as if nothing had happened. But I couldn't understand how you couldn't want to see or know, especially after having my children, I couldn't understand it, when the opportunity was there, for her not to take it.❞

We know much less about the impact of the experience on those who do the rejecting. Fraser, who spoke above, had a single meeting with his brother, clearly felt troubled by the impact. Similarly Charlotte, who had a single meeting with her birth mother, also continued to feel guilty, saying 'I've felt guilty about it ever since – which makes me very cross because I don't see why I should – but I can't get rid of it – I do still feel guilty about it.' It is quite possible that some rejecting birth relatives have similar feelings.

While the initial feelings of hurt and confusion are common, over the longer term there is variation in how adopted people react to rejection. Some people respond by coming out fighting, others take refuge by focusing on other things. We shall now look at these 'fight' and 'flight' responses before examining the ways in which people are able eventually to come to terms with their birth relative's unwillingness to continue with contact.

Fight and flight

Rejection is a hurtful experience. A natural response is to hit back if someone hurts us. One way in which many people deal with rejection is by getting angry. They want to hit back and hurt. Cheryl had approached her birth mother via an intermediary but her birth mother rejected all contact. Here is Cheryl's response:

> ❝I thought 'stuff her'. The childish bit in me used to phone her up every birthday and put the phone down five or six times a day just to wind her up and think 'you won't bloody forget today'. That lasted a couple of years, it was quite pathetic really but never mind. I did sit outside the house one day. I didn't have the courage to do any more than that. I'm quite angry towards her – I am still. I've got this rational side of me that says 'yes but . . . ' but I've got this angry side that says 'bitch'. Why didn't she just say 'I'll meet you once'? Nobody needed to know. I could acknowledge that it was difficult for her, that she had other children, that maybe her husband made it difficult as well. I could acknowledge that she probably had a really hard time of it. But I couldn't understand how you couldn't want to see or know me, especially as I have also had children. So I feel very mixed. I don't feel like it's finished. I haven't finished yet. I almost want to hurt her now – that sounds horrible doesn't it? No it's not finished and that leaves me in limbo.❞

Cheryl acknowledges that her own reaction might be seen as 'childish'. But the anger she describes is an understandable natural reaction to the hurt she experienced. There was no way that she could suppress it. What she reacted to was the pain of the rejection, her inability to understand why it had happened, which led to further frustration and a desire for revenge. While anger is a natural and sometimes healthy response to hurt, taking steps to punish the other person does not always help. It does not take account of the reasons why the other person chose not to meet you or respond. As we have seen, these reactions can often arise out of fear rather than heartlessness. Trying to hurt the other person is unlikely to produce a positive response and is not likely to help you to move on. It might even keep you 'in limbo'. This was Cheryl's experience. The key is to find a way of directing your anger and then let it go. This may take time and you may find that it helps to talk to someone – a friend or a counsellor. We shall say more about this later.

The alternative to fighting is to flee. We saw earlier how a lack of a clearly welcoming response means that some people take flight rather than stay around and risk rejection. In Elizabeth's case she took the running metaphor quite literally:

> ❝I decided that I would write a letter to her. I wanted her to know that everything had worked out for the best. I can certainly remember reassuring her that I wasn't going to keep contacting her. I was quite frightened that a letter like this coming out of the blue she might drop dead of a heart attack. I never expected a reply. I wasn't writing the letter to receive a letter back. Having said that, when I heard that she had received my letter, and that she was not going to reply, that was quite hard to deal with.

Although I never expected to receive anything, knowing that she wasn't going to was, well, I suppose it was a rejection really. I know logically why she didn't and why she hasn't and it's probably just as well she hasn't but at the time it was a bit of a slap in the face. I've always assumed that she's wondered about me, now perhaps she hasn't, I don't know, I've no idea. I suppose I found I felt this rejection and I hadn't expected to. I perhaps hadn't admitted to myself perhaps I was secretly hoping that a letter would come. Perhaps what I had expected was 'how wonderful to hear from you, I've always thought about you blah blah blah . . . ' and of course I didn't get that. So I dealt with that by running! I say that joking but I was running, and I then went off and ran the marathon. I actually did start running quite seriously. I mean, the feelings went away after a while. I think I probably contained them, yeah. Well plus I'd got the children to look after and life was going on. I don't want it to sound as if it were a major crisis. It wasn't, it was upsetting and it was something that I hadn't expected and was something that I had to come to terms with. I think you just get on with it. I'm not a great thinker, and I'm not a great dweller. **"**

Elizabeth's response was the direct opposite of Cheryl's. As she says, it is her natural way of dealing with things, not by getting angry or upset but by not dwelling on the situation and focusing on other things. The downside of this approach is that feelings of hurt and rejection get buried; they are still there, but covered over. That is not to say we recommend that everyone starts to unleash their anger, but we do think that it can sometimes help to explore your feelings before putting them away.

Strategies for dealing with rejection

If you experience a rejection you will have to find ways to look after yourself. The rejection is likely to be painful, although many adopted people in our study were able to come to terms with it and move on. Here are some of the strategies that people used which they felt worked for them.

Being prepared

Before you start out on a reunion try to make yourself as ready as possible. Make sure you feel fine about yourself. Try to think through every possibility – what if the other person does not respond at all; what if you are rejected after a single meeting? What if you meet them and do not want to take it any further? If you do not feel ready to deal with these possibilities, then protect yourself by waiting a little longer.

Directing anger

If you are rejected try to find positive ways of expressing and then letting go of your anger. Try not to bury your anger and hurt, but equally don't use your anger to hit out at someone.

Reaching an understanding

As part of the process, try to make sense of why the rejection might have happened. You might have been given a reason by the other person. It is probably worth thinking about what might lie behind the reason you have been given. You might find that some of our quotes from birth mothers, and from adopted people who rejected or were rejected, can help you to try to understand motivations.

Meeting another relative

In some cases a rejection by one birth relative is also accompanied by a full reunion with another. Inevitably, being accepted by one birth relative does help. It is important, however, that you still work through the initial rejection.

Identifying the positives

Although rejection is a painful experience it does not necessarily make the whole search and reunion process invalid. In our research, 90 per cent of those who experienced a rejection said they had no regrets about searching for and trying to make contact with their birth parent. This is not simply trying to make the best of a bad job. Three-quarters of people said that although they did not establish a relationship with their birth relative, they still felt that the search had helped to answer important questions about their background.

Equally, some people felt that the important thing was to have tried, even though it did not work out; as Cora says:

> ❝I've said this before, but I'll say it again, I don't have any regrets at all about trying to trace my natural mother. I have no regrets at all about getting access to my original birth record and having all that information. The fact is that I tried and therefore there isn't that niggling 'well maybe if had . . . or maybe she . . .'. I think it must be very hard for people who don't try, don't try, don't try and then they do try and they died last week, or something like that.❞

Having and getting support

Probably the most important thing is to make sure that you do not have to deal with the rejection alone. Michael had to deal with a double rejection from both his birth mother and birth father, but he was able to draw on a lot of support:

> ❝No, no regrets. It was hard work emotionally whilst it was going on, it was certainly hard work when the rejection came again. It ended up being more difficult with my father than with my mother. I don't regret it, if anything it's filled in a lot of blanks for me and I know a lot more about me. But the time for me was right, because I've got the stability of a wife and a family and my adoptive parents, and that whole thing is so

strong whatever came out of it, I was going to be all right. I'd be able to handle it, so no, I don't regret it. I would have regretted not doing it at some point so I'm pleased I did it. Losses are the rollercoaster, went to the bottom of the ride again for a short space of time, but that's more than outweighed by what I managed to find out. Even though I didn't meet them, just to know where they live, know a bit more about it, things that I didn't realise. **"**

Friends and family can be invaluable supports. But you may well want to get additional help, particularly from other people who have been in the same situation who may be part of a support group, or from an experienced counsellor. This is Cora's statement:

"She had sent a letter, my natural mother, saying that I wasn't her daughter as far as she was concerned, and please not to contact her. So I came in and talked to the intermediary quite a lot about that and I started seeing a therapist for a bit as well. . . . Angry, very very very angry. . . . I wouldn't discourage anybody from trying, but I would ask that anybody who tries to trace is supported by a professional body and by people that are outside of their adoptive family and outside their circle of friends. **"**

Summary

- Few adopted people are rejected outright or even after one or two contacts. Equally, few adopted people reject an approach from a birth relative.

- Although rejection does not happen very often, it is important to think about how you might feel and how you would cope with it before embarking on a reunion.

- There are all kinds of reasons why rejection occurs – the main ones seem to be when people have kept the adoption secret or moved on and say they do not feel any emotional connection.

- The experience of rejection is painful, but you can come to terms with it. What seems to help most is trying to make sense of why it might have happened, identifying the positives from the search process, and having support to help you to deal with your feelings.

The search and reunion journey

9

In this chapter we discuss the search and reunion journey as a whole, highlighting the possible gains as well as the challenges.

Introduction

Previous chapters have traced the highs and lows of reunion, the moments of joy as well as frustration, the triumphs and setbacks, reunions that work and reunions that founder. Search and reunion is a long journey, from first thoughts about making contact through to the first meeting (if it happens), and on into the years beyond. Inevitably, it is also an emotional journey, one where you cannot predict how or where you might end up. In this chapter we reflect on the search and reunion journey as a whole. We are careful not to talk about any specific destinations – it will be obvious by now that all reunions are different and everyone's experience is unique. But we do look at what influences the journey, what you might get out of it, and some of the things that will help you on your way.

For most people the search and reunion process is an emotional rollercoaster. Even so, the great majority of people in our research were pleased that they had done it. In all, 85 per cent of searchers and 72 per cent of adopted people who had been searched for said that the reunion had been a positive experience. This high approval rating might come as something of a surprise given some of the difficult issues that we have high-lighted in earlier chapters, especially those who have experienced a rejection. You might think that some of the adopted people in our survey were either fooling themselves or simply putting on a brave face. We do not think that is the case. Most people are realistic enough, or become realistic enough, to recognise that reunions are not about fairy-tale endings. A few reunions are easy from the beginning, some have tough patches, and a few stutter badly from the start. Whatever happens along the way, there are three key things that you might expect from your journey: information about your roots, relationships with others, and a rite of passage (a new way of feeling and thinking about yourself). We'll look at each of these in turn.

Roots

Whatever happens, a bonus for most people is that they normally get a much stronger and clearer picture of who they are and where they have come from. As Susan said:

> **❝**I used to very much feel as I was growing up like I'd just been plonked on the earth – a mystery, no past at all that you can relate to – so you feel isolated and cut-off. I'm sure that's one of the reasons why wanting to find birth parents is so important because it makes you have a beginning, a middle and an end.**❞**

And similarly for Kenneth:

> **❝**I feel my life's more complete now, it's that missing link that's always been at the back of your mind. Like the missing pieces have just been put in the jigsaw.**❞**

Our own survey found that around 80 per cent of adopted people said the search and reunion process helped them to answer important questions about their origins and background. Having access to the birth records gave most people the chance to fill in missing parts of their story with details of names, characteristics and circumstances. A strong sense of roots and family history can come from simply reading the adoption record. But for many people it was only meeting a birth relative that enabled a fuller picture to emerge and a real sense of connection to be established. We were struck by the number of interviewees who were bowled over by meeting for the first time someone who looked like them, and by people who discovered shared mannerisms or personality traits and even shared likes and dislikes. People who grow up with their birth families take all this for granted, but for adopted people it is one of the most rewarding parts of the reunion journey. It is also one that does not depend so much on how the reunion works out. It is possible to gain a clearer picture about your background, even if the reunion is difficult.

Relationships with others

The second possible gain from a reunion are new relationships with birth relatives, and for some, confirmation of the importance of their relationship with their adoptive parents and family. However, as we have seen, working out new relationships can sometimes be a more difficult 'reward' to achieve than gaining knowledge about your roots.

It can be a real challenge to build a relationship with each new relative. You will have a biological tie in common but in other respects you are strangers. The reunion often involves trying to establish a 'family' relationship in a short period of time when you are an adult rather than a child. Working out the relationship can be complicated by feelings of rejection, loss and anger.

Another reason why adoption reunions are challenging journeys is the number of individual relationships that need to be developed, or maybe reworked as a result of the reunion: with your birth mother, birth father, birth siblings, other birth relatives, adoptive parents, adoptive siblings, and perhaps your relationship with your partner and children. You will also have to work out how they all fit together, and discover if you can fit them all into your life. On one level this can simply be about finding the time for everyone, as Kate describes:

> **❝**The first 18 months were crucifying, trying to see everybody – my birth mother, my half-siblings, I've got my [adoptive] parents, I'd got my parents' family, I'd got friends who wanted to know what was going on. I think every weekend we felt obliged to do something, or see someone. We were invited somewhere and it was 'oh we'll have to go – if we don't what will they think?' Eventually I ran out of steam. You work through this, you finally get to think 'I can't do this any more – I've got to stop'. And we did. We didn't have a particular point – we just suddenly stopped. I think I just gave in. And of course in the natural course of things, everything has settled down.**❞**

Working out how everyone connects and meets up is about much more than time. What you have to negotiate is whether and how you belong to each family, and this will often raise issues of belonging and not belonging as well as raise feelings of conflict of loyalty. There may also be the question of how your three, possibly four, families fit together or overlap. Here then, are some of the relationship challenges you *may* have to face:

- The other person is not committed to the reunion, or as committed as you, leaving you feeling frustrated, let down or rejected.
- You feel your feelings are not being taken into account and you feel that you are being taken advantage of, or dumped on, by a family member.
- You don't feel fully part of the birth mother or birth father's family.
- The other person is too committed, leaving you feeling overwhelmed or maybe guilty if you keep them at arm's length.
- It feels like others are competing for you, or that you are in competition with others, whether birth or adoptive parents, partners or siblings. You might find that your loyalties are torn, or that you are trying to please everyone.
- You only get on with some birth family members, not all.
- You feel overwhelmed by the intense emotions stirred up by the reunion concerning adoption, childhood, or simply managing the reunion itself.
- You find that you don't have anything in common with the birth relatives; you don't like them, or you have lost interest in the reunion.
- Your reunion is with a birth relative who has personal problems such as mental health difficulties or an addiction.
- Simply finding the time and emotional energy to accommodate all these new people in your life is difficult.

- There may be resentment by people with whom you have an established relationship (parents, siblings, partner, friends) that you are excited and have taken up with your new relationships, and they may feel rejected.

This is by no means an exhaustive list of all the things that can test you. We have not produced the list to put you off, but as a way to prepare you for what might lie ahead. Any reunion is going to be about getting on with real people rather than the people you might hope to meet. At some stage most reunions face one or more of the challenges listed above. In most cases these challenges are worked around and worked through, given time. In the remainder of this section we look at some of these issues in more depth and make some suggestions for tackling problem areas, although some issues are inherently difficult and you may end up just having to live with them.

Relationship challenges 1: Rights and entitlements

Family members have all sorts of rights and obligations to each other. In other words they know what they can expect, more or less. In non-adoptive families people will have gradually built up expectations of each other, covering issues such as who phones who and how often, or who pays for what. When you are joining a new family, you have to work out these understandings from the beginning, and there are bound to be times when there are different expectations and assumptions. All kinds of apparently everyday issues might cause confusion or tension. For example, how often you see each other, whether you have a right to be told about holiday plans or illnesses and accidents, and whether you should send a 'from your son/daughter' card on birthdays, or receive one to 'my daughter'.

These 'minor' issues can prove difficult, adding to that feeling of being an outsider. Or you might feel you are being taken advantage of but do not have the confidence and security in your new family to express how you feel. Ann, for example, found it hard at first to set firm boundaries with her sister:

> ❝I started to feel as if I was being used. It's almost as if because she now had an older sister she felt as if she could just borrow all my clothes, use the phone and everything. I started to think to myself 'I've got to stand up for myself here in this, because I mean she may be my sister but I'm not going to be treated like this'. I felt as if I was obliged to give in because I had found them so I should be eternally grateful. It was difficult the first year and I felt really shy and pathetic and stuff.❞

There is no easy way around these issues of rights and responsibilities. Most people work them out over time as they settle into a pattern of relating. Perhaps the two most useful ways to deal with these difficulties are to talk them through and be realistic about what you should expect from the relationship in the early stages. For example, Zara reflected:

> ❝I want to push her [birth mother] a bit more to find out a few more things – but again it is only a year. For instance, before she went on holiday she didn't actually ring

me to say she was going. I did get a postcard when she was out there. But you can't suddenly change your life and put someone else altogether into it. **"**

Relationship challenges 2: Parity of commitment

The easiest reunions tend to be those where both sides place roughly equal importance on the relationship. Sometimes this can be very low key or it can be fairly intense. But there can be problems in birth mother and birth father reunions where one side is much more committed and zealous about the reunion than the other, leaving one side feeling hurt, rejected or let down, and the other feeling pressured, guilty or pursued. It is possible to work around some imbalances in the relationship, particularly if you can talk them through a little.

Relationship challenges 3: Roles and names

Another challenge is to work out what role the new family member is to play in your life. This is often easier with siblings as they can take on the status of a 'friend' or simply be another brother or sister. It is not always so easy with birth mothers and fathers, given that most adopted people still have a mother and father. The question then is, what roles are the birth mother or father to play – an extra mother/father, a friend, or something else? And what should they be called?

Adopted people approach this issue in different ways. Whether or not the birth parent is seen as or called 'mother' or 'father' does not necessarily relate to how well they get on with them. Sally, for example, had a close relationship with her birth mother but did not consider her to have taken on the 'mother' role:

"I've got a far better relationship with my birth mother in a lot of ways than I have with my adoptive mother, but it's not complicated by the mother/daughter thing in other ways. It's strange, it's a unique relationship. But then again in other ways it's going to be less rich isn't it, because of the lack of shared experience? So there isn't that, but it's rich in other ways. It's rich in ways that move forward if you like, rather than look back. **"**

For other people, however, it just feels natural to call the birth parent 'mother' or 'mum', as in Dawn's case:

"It started off with 'Angela' and then something clicked and I just called her 'Mum'. It gets confusing, especially if I'm talking to friends about it because I call my mother-in-law and father-in-law 'Mum' and 'Dad'. So I've got three sets of Mums and Dads. They get really confused and they say 'well which one?' and I say 'oh yeah, sorry'. So I have to explain. **"**

What to call the birth parent can be difficult and confusing, although the confusion over names can be a great source of fun. Sometimes adoptive parents feel hurt by the birth parent being referred to as 'mum or dad' as they may feel their position and status as the primary parent is under threat. For others this does not present a problem – we might compare it to when people get married, some in-laws may be called mum and dad. This is a sensitive area and an ideal situation is when everyone respects the feelings and wishes of others, and finds a solution with which everyone is comfortable. A few birth mothers make things easier by being quite clear that they do not want or expect to be called 'Mum', as Owen explains:

> **❝**I call her by her first name. Which is Ann. She said at the very beginning 'I gave birth to you but your Mum brought you up – so don't call me Mum, call me Ann' – and I said 'that's great – that's exactly what I wanted to hear' – because I didn't want Mum thinking that she'd been replaced.**❞**

Relationship challenges 4: Genetic sexual attraction

By far the most uncomfortable and sensitive issue in reunions is when roles become blurred and reunion participants are sexually attracted to each other. The issue of 'genetic sexual attraction' has received a lot of sensational coverage in the newspapers. We have not mentioned it so far in the individual chapters on reunions with birth mothers, fathers and siblings because it is an issue that cuts across all reunions. Although it is a difficult topic, we think it is essential that people are forewarned.

If this is the first time you have heard of genetic sexual attraction you may be surprised and shocked. However, as we have seen, reunions can evoke very strong emotions. Usually these feelings are not sexual but they are intense. They can also be difficult to understand or put a name to, simply because as adults we normally only expect to have such strong and immediate emotions in the context of a romantic relationship. Because of this, sometimes the language of reunions draws on that of adult romantic relationships – the 'honeymoon' phase, for example – just because we do not have any other words to describe it. And some of our interviewees also compared their sudden feeling of closeness to similar experiences with romantic partners. Eleanor's reunion with her birth mother is an example where she likens the sudden rush of feelings to being in love:

> **❝**Very, very emotional – we just kept looking at each other – it was really, really strange. It was like a magnet. I just kept looking at her and I suppose she just kept looking at me – noticing things. I just felt very close. It's hard to describe the feeling. The nearest thing is when you're in love with somebody, it's that sort of tense feeling and closeness.**❞**

Some of our interviewees also commented on the strangeness of suddenly forging a close relationship with an adult stranger, as Harry remembers:

> **❝**We brought my sister home that evening and we actually sat up all night. My wife went to bed and that felt very strange in itself, sitting with this strange girl who was my sister, you know sort of almost arm in arm sort of thing, and there was my wife

going off to bed, and I'm thinking 'well hang on a minute, this is really strange'. This woman in the house, even though she was my sister. **"**

For Eleanor and Harry, and indeed for most of our interviewees, the intensity of feelings can be hard to describe but they do not necessarily have any clear sexual element. However, in a few cases, the intensity of feelings *did* take on a sexual tone, but prior warnings by adoption counsellors meant that the reunion participants were able to deal with it, as happened in David's reunion with his birth mother:

"We did go through a phase of when we had all these mixed emotions and because she's not married I think she assumed I was the role of like a son and the only man in her life as well, which was very confusing. Now we're supposed to know each other very well, but we don't, we're strangers. And I said to her that I'd been to the counsellor and they did mention this. And then she said 'well I wasn't going to say anything but I have had those feelings' and she got all confused about what I am really, I suppose. And she said, and this is like a year afterwards, 'I'm glad you had the gumption to say that these feelings might happen, because I was having those feelings'. It's a very difficult thing to do I suppose. But you should continue doing that [raising it as an issue in counselling] I think, even though it's a dodgy subject. **"**

No one knows why genetic sexual attraction occurs, but a number of different factors are likely to be involved – the intense feelings generated in the reunion, the lack of a shared family experience which means that clear boundaries have not been set up, maybe the attraction of physical similarity and finding that you have a lot in common, or your birth parent finding that you look just like your father or mother now that you are the age they were when you were conceived. Sometimes sexual feelings occur because people are perhaps trying to make up for the lost opportunity to bond and be physically close to a baby or parent. What is clear from David's account is, firstly, the importance of being alerted beforehand, but also the importance of acknowledging the attraction if it occurs and then talking it through together, no matter how odd or uncomfortable it feels. It can be difficult if you are in this situation, but talking about what is going on, or thinking about the best way to handle your feelings, might suggest ways to deal with it. And if it all feels too confusing and out of control, a frank discussion might at least break some of the power of what is happening between you.

It is unclear how common genetic sexual attraction is. There have been alarmist media reports suggesting that it happens a great deal. In our study this was not the case. It was more likely that people felt confused about how to treat a 'close stranger' than to have a clear sexual attraction. Nevertheless, sometimes a full sexual relationship does develop. We met one case and we include it here to give an idea of how it happens and some of the complications that the brother and sister experienced:

"There was quite a big attraction with the second brother I met. And we carried on writing. Then he divorced and came to live near here. All purely platonic then. And it ended up with me leaving my husband. There was nobody else. But within a couple of months we both admitted what we felt and then it was 'what do you do?' This is when The Children's Society came into play, because I went and saw someone about it and she was amazed that nobody had warned me when the search began that it was one of the things that could happen. And I'd not felt anything for my other brother, so there was no inkling that it could happen. So I was quite taken aback when I found out that it was happening. We then had to decide whether we kept up a sham as half brother and sister, or whether we said we were lovers. Do we come out like the gays did? That's what it's amounted to in the end. And as soon as my ex twigged what was happening he was on the phone threatening me with whatever he could to get me behind bars. My birth mother eventually found out and didn't want anything to do with us any more. She blames me for having brought everybody together and now ripping everyone apart. And she wanted us in jail as well. **"**

Relationship challenges 5: Finding common ground

A more comfortable, but still difficult challenge for some reunions is trying to find some common ground. It is not unusual for adopted people to have been brought up in a different lifestyle from that of their birth family. This is a particular issue for people of mixed ethnicity who have been adopted by white families. Of course many non-adopted people move away from their families culturally and educationally, but they have a shared history to draw upon. It can be difficult meeting a stranger who is very different from you in terms of class, culture or even generation and when all you have in common is a blood tie. But given time it is possible to find things in common, particularly if you are able to see the positives, despite differences. Zara gives an example:

> **"**I didn't feel really at home because they are not anything like the family that I was brought up with. But I knew they were quite normal – welcoming – they made an effort. **"**

It can also be demanding when you attempt to build a relationship with a birth relative who has major personal difficulties such as an addiction or mental health problem. It can be very hard to establish a meaningful and positive relationship in such situations, but if you can appreciate the strengths as well as the weaknesses of the other person, it is possible to establish common ground. For example, Kim explained:

> **"**She's not without her own difficulties – she's a manic depressive. And she has never got over giving me away, and she will say that. And when I was post-natally depressed I could talk to her for hours about things like that and now I've put it behind me and she hasn't. I don't think she's ever going to move from that. I've got to accept that. But there's an emotional bond there. But I've got to realise she's a damaged individual and she's quite fragile so I've got to watch what I put on her. But we can talk about everything and anything. I mean we can talk about her boyfriend – we won't reach an agreement on it, but we can talk about it. **"**

You might find that you have very little in common with a birth relative, or simply do not get on. There are some factors – different backgrounds and personal problems especially – that can make it more difficult, but not impossible to find common ground. Give the relationship time to develop if you can as it could become an important part in your life. However, we recognise that, just as in any family, some people get on and others do not. If this is the case then, having shared facts and feelings, the contact might either ease off or simply peter out.

Relationship challenges 6: Anger

It is unusual for a child to be given up by a birth parent. Because it is uncommon and against the 'natural' way of things, we all need to find some reason to explain why it happened, possibly to hold someone, or something, to account. For some people this is a live issue before the reunion. Yasmin, for example, recalls feeling anger and hate towards her birth mother as a child:

> **“**I think I used to hate her for it. Even though I wanted to meet her and stuff, I think I wanted to meet her so I could have my say – because to a certain extent I feel like she, not ruined my life, but she had a big part in why my life is the way that it is.**”**

Other people do not feel angry (or are unaware of feeling angry) with their birth mothers at the beginning, but become angry at a later stage. This anger is usually shown because adopted people find it hard to accept the reasons for the adoption or understand that the birth mother had genuinely no choice other than to place the child for adoption. Jacob, for example, only felt angry later in the reunion when he had his own child. He questioned how his own mother could have given him away:

> **“**I was always surprised I wasn't more angry with her – I was always shocked that when I met her I hadn't been angry – but I wasn't. I never felt a strong sense of anger until my daughter was born. That's the first time I started to genuinely feel angry – I had a word with her about it a month or two ago and she cried and said that she was actually pleased because she felt I had to be angry – so there's that thing about being a bit annoyed, a bit angry – whatever it is.**”**

It is not always the birth mother towards whom people feel angry, or hold responsible for placing them for adoption. As we saw in Chapter 5, the sense of blame and responsibility can be placed on the birth father for abandoning the birth mother. Sometimes blame is directed at the maternal birth grandparents for not supporting their daughter, and at other times the adoptive parents, or occasionally society in general rather than a particular individual.

So how do you deal with anger? The key is to be honest about your feelings and talk to your birth relative, or counsellor, about how you are feeling and why. It might be worth thinking about what might have happened if you had not been placed for adoption (see

'Reaching reality or realism' below). What would have been the circumstances? It is impossible to know exactly how things might have been, but you could think through those things that might have been easier and those that might have been harder for your birth parent. The reality is that you cannot change what happened. Meeting birth relatives might help you to come to terms with the situation, no matter how your adoption has worked out.

When you do attempt to discuss matters with your birth parents, you might find that they will not answer your questions. Or you might be reluctant to ask questions or you might struggle to accept the answers given. Trust your feelings. As we have seen, one of the things that the reunion can offer is the opportunity to ask questions. Nicola describes her need to ask lots of questions, even though she was not always content with the answers:

> **❝**And even to this day I still don't accept her reasons [for the adoption]. I think over a long period of time perhaps acceptance will be there. The more I know about her the more she's gone into detail with things and the more I find out. The fact that I've been able to ask questions that I've wanted to ask whether I accept them or not is down to me.**❞**

Relationship challenges 7: Fear of rejection

The last relationship challenge we look at is a fear of rejection. Earlier chapters have shown that a fear of rejection can be present many years into a reunion, and that such fear can influence how the relationship develops in different ways. We saw in Chapter 4 how some people try to protect themselves by not showing their feelings first and hoping for, or trying to provoke, an expression of love from their birth mothers in indirect ways. In other cases adopted people try to keep the relationship under their control. Nicola explained:

> **❝**I've got what I want, it's on my terms. I've dictated to her the way things have gone. When I started this I didn't want a relationship, whether I was trying to protect myself from being rejected once more I don't know. But I've found her and she's accepted me more than I've accepted her.**❞**

In other cases, particularly with birth mother reunions, the adopted person avoided talking about difficult issues such as the circumstances of the adoption for fear of disrupting a new and potentially fragile relationship. And some people who had felt initially welcomed by birth relatives, but then felt as if their 'novelty' value had worn off, did feel rejected and returned once more to their adoptive family.

Establishing a new relationship with birth relatives takes courage. You are putting yourself on the line with no guarantees that your birth relatives will reciprocate or commit themselves to building a relationship. Perhaps the only way forward is to try to talk it over, not accusing the other of not caring or not caring enough, but instead saying that you do not always feel you can ask for more contact or ask the other person how she would like the relationship to develop. Sometimes your feelings of rejection may just reflect your own feelings of uncertainty in the new relationship, or a sense that the other person has a lot of other things going on in her life, as Dawn found:

> **"**Sometimes I get the feeling that she's got in contact and that's it – she don't want to know any more – but then you get a phone call and she's all bubbly – you go up again. It's hard for her to get in contact and I work and it's such a long way – sometimes I feel like she don't want to know me anymore. But she'll say 'you stupid girl' – I shan't say what she really says! But yeah she reassures me and I say 'oh yeah, it's just me'.**"**

If you are able to have that conversation and find that the other person is not heavily committed to the relationship, then you can adjust your expectations. You can then decide how and where you want to go from there.

Rite of passage (or the relationship with yourself)

So far, we have looked at two possible things you can get out of the search and reunion process. Most people gain an appreciation of their 'roots'. Many people establish or rework relationships with others, which can be a very challenging part of the journey. But perhaps the most important relationship you can build is the one with yourself – strengthen your sense of self and who you are. By undertaking the search and reunion journey you might come to terms with a range of questions and issues to do with being adopted, your identity, and how you connect with other people, including and especially your adoptive and birth families. No matter how the relationship works out with your birth relatives you are unlikely to come out unchanged as a person, as Lucy discovered:

> **"**I feel like I'm just like on one great big huge sort of learning process. I'm glad that I've done it and I'm really glad that I've found her and I'm glad of everything that's happened so far. But more to do with how it's affected like me personally, internally, rather than in relationship with her. I've felt that's helped me understand better the effects of having been adopted in my life and having found out more about my adoption than anything personal to do with my birth mother. I've gained information that has helped me make sense of my feelings and I suppose it's shed light on aspects of my life that mean I've been able to understand myself better.**"**

The reunion experience can therefore be a real rite of passage, enabling you to make sense of what being given up for adoption and growing up in a different family means to you. It is likely to help to answer questions of who you are and where you come from. It will probably clarify how you relate to your birth and adoptive families. These may be questions that you think about at the beginning of the search, or they might be raised only when you are well into your search. Indeed, quite a few people are taken by surprise about how much the search and reunion process stirs up feelings they had not realised they had. Kay, for example had never been particularly interested in her adoption, but found herself deeply affected when, after she had been contacted by a birth sibling, she found out her birth mother had died:

> ❝Until this letter came I'd never thought about it. I've always felt happy. But the letter made me start thinking 'well, where did I come from?' The fact that I'd found out that my birth mother had passed away sent me to pieces for these two years. And I couldn't understand my feelings – 'why was I breaking down when I'd had no desire to go and find her, why did it shake me up so much?'❞

Irene also found herself taken aback by the strength of her feelings when she started her search:

> ❝When I first came to the adopted people's workshop I really hadn't spoken about it very much and I found it very emotional, very draining. I was crying and it was really a shock for me to realise how emotive it was in me. I hadn't realised how I felt about it really. So being forced to talk about it in groups of people – it brings a lot of your emotions to the surface I think, which you don't deal with day-to-day. It makes you come to terms with a few more things – makes you have to sit down and think why you are searching, or what you really want from this.❞

The process can raise a lot of emotional issues which you have to tackle. For most people this is going to be a worthwhile journey – a majority of searchers in our research said they felt 'more complete' as a person after their reunion. But at times it will be a hard road to tread. Although most people feel positive overall about their reunion, for some the gains are tempered by the need to cope with some strong and testing feelings.

The importance of expectations

Some of the major influences on how your journey begins are your hopes and expectations. Most people try to work out with their adoption counsellor what their expectations should be, but it is not always easy to predict what you really might be looking for beforehand, as Jenny found:

> ❝I suppose the worst thing is that it hasn't been like the fairytale, delightful, this person who I completely click with. Not that I consciously had those expectations, but now I've done it I guess they must have been to some degree. If I had absolutely my perfect ideal scene, which was like a fantasy, it would be that she would write me like nice letters saying you know how much she loved me and tell me things about what it was like then and you know stuff like that, and I would feel important to her and loved by her.❞

Jenny's story also highlights how you might hope for a 'roses around the door' or a perfect reunion with 'perfect parents' who will meet all your needs. Of course everyone wants things to go well, but having what is called an 'anastrophic' expectation – that is, an unrealistic expectation or fantasy that cannot be realised – can lead to big disappointments as the reunion unfolds. Equally, the opposite position of having catastrophic expectations, or assuming the worst will happen, can also prevent you from either starting out on the process or fully committing yourself to the reunion.

As expectations can shape the reunion process it is worth trying to be as clear as you can be about your expectations and whether or not they are realistic. As we have seen from Jenny it can be hard to pinpoint your expectations beforehand. Even so, it is important to try to work them out as much as possible before you begin. We have some suggestions about how to do this. But at the same time one of the great (and also difficult!) things about reunions is that they are journeys in which you cannot predict at the beginning how things are going to turn out and how you are going to feel or grow. The trick, if there is one, is to approach the reunion with an open mind and in a spirit of curiosity.

Reaching reality or realism

Just as the reunion is likely to raise issues about adoption, identity and family for you, the reunion is also likely to be the way in which you come to terms with these experiences. Getting information about your background and building a relationship with a birth relative can give you a much stronger sense of your roots. It adds to your sense of identity. But by itself, a reunion with a birth relative will not make you complete or meet all your emotional needs. You cannot rely on another individual to provide these things. Ultimately they can only come from within. What the reunion can really do, however, is help you to work through and come to terms with your adoption, including who you are and why you were placed. As Olive found:

> ❝I thought when I met my mum everything would be in place, all my insecurities would go into check, my whole life would be sorted. And all it did was bring up more questions with less answers. I think most children still want this perfect family and it doesn't exist. But even before I met her I realised you are what you are. There isn't a magic pill, a magic formula, a magic family that comes along and stops you feeling the way you do about yourself.❞

Part of the journey, or the rite of passage, is to let go of any remaining fantasies about the birth family – either as the bad guys or as possible saviours. You will not know what might have been if you had not been adopted, but the chances are that by finding out about your birth family you may get a more realistic picture of what life might have been like, as Kim recognised:

> ❝I can remember my birth mother said she went home and told my grandmother 'I've met Kim and Kim's a doctor and she's a bright girl. Isn't that wonderful? I should have kept her.' And my grandmother turned round to her and said 'Well she probably wouldn't have been a doctor if she'd stayed with you because of what you could have

given her'. I might have done, I might not have done. But my life would have been very difficult and there probably would have been a series of uncles, because nobody in those days would have wanted to take on a young woman with a kid. You know there isn't always the roses round the door ending. **”**

The challenges of the reunion process may also help to achieve a more realistic and balanced picture of your adoptive family. As with most parents, few adoptive parents in our study handled everything well all of the time. Some had not been particularly open about the adoption. Not a few struggled with the reunion process. Also, like any other parents, they might be perceived as having been too strict, too distant, or too suffocating. Meeting your birth relatives can help you to reflect on your adoption, acknowledging the good parts as well as the difficult bits. It might offer you the chance to sort out any outstanding issues with your adoptive parents.

Sometimes relationships with your adoptive parents are relieved of a certain strain or angst once you have contacted your birth family and addressed issues to do with your adoption. Una, for example, is a person of mixed ethnicity who had a very positive reunion experience with her black birth family. She is firmly convinced that black and mixed ethnicity children should be placed with black families, but her own personal reunion journey helped her to appreciate just what she had obtained from her white adoptive family:

“I suppose the loss would be the loss of the fantasy I had built up about my birth family. And if I look at it truthfully I am different. I'm very different to my father in personality and in outlook. And I'm quite different to my sister in outlook although in personality we are quite the same. I really do believe that I wouldn't be who I was today if I hadn't have been adopted. Knowing my birth family I don't think I would have studied, gone to university. I don't think I would have had the same outlook on life. I think the way that I was brought up has made me a deep thinker, has made me challenge, has made me look. And so I can't say that I feel I would have been better off if I'd stayed. I'm now satisfied with who I am and what I am. And I think those are the painful things that you have to go through. You have to come to terms with the fact that life is not a fantasy and it's not a rehearsal. It's what you get – you have to deal with what you've got and you have to be satisfied. I think sometimes when I was going through the identity issue I'd think 'why can't I be brought up in a black family . . . ?' and now I look back on it and I think 'well OK that might have happened but you wouldn't be Una, you wouldn't be who you are – you wouldn't have anything that you've got now'. And I do feel now that I am blessed. I do have a lot to be thankful for and that's one of the reasons why I wrote to my [adoptive] mother to say 'thank you'. So you've got to take that on board. You can't be resentful about that. You've got to put that aside and look at it sensibly and move on from that and take what you've got from it and just accept it really. I think that's what it's about, it's about finding the acceptance and balance and I think that's what I've managed, hopefully managed, to do. **”**

The third area of 'reality-reaching' is about the reunion itself. None of the reunions in our study was perfect. Some were wonderful but none was entirely problem-free. Reunions pose challenging prospects. It is important to prepare yourself for possible struggles along the way and to accept that ideals and reality rarely coincide. Zara, for example, was in the early stage of her reunion and was experiencing some frustrations but realised that they were inevitable:

> **❝**She hasn't opened up as much as I want her to about some things but it's only early days. But sometimes it niggles me and my partner will say 'please, just take it easy' and is quite good at making me look at the way she's feeling. So I think it's going to be OK the way things are going. Sometimes, I've thought I might give the adoption counsellor a ring just to say 'is it natural to be annoyed sometimes?' But I know that really. I know that it is.**❞**

Or, here is Wendy, much further down the road, and yet still experiencing some problems though she feels very satisfied overall with how things were going. Crucially, she accepts that some bits of the reunion were never going to work out as she hoped:

> **❝**If I had a wish I would just wish my husband and my birth mother got on really well. But we can get round that. They don't spend a lot of time in each other's company and when they do they are pretty good with each other. Nothing in a reunion is ever going to be perfect and that is the one bit that has been difficult. But it's probably the only bit, apart from sorting through my own emotions which I'm probably about 85 per cent of the way there with now.**❞**

Some reunions are much more of a struggle than Zara or Wendy's. Some people experience rejection and do not even have a reunion. But what you can gain for yourself and your development does not depend on how well the relationship works out with other people. The opposite might be the case. A reunion where you have had real struggles can end up strengthened. An emotionally demanding reunion can produce the greatest reflection and personal growth. So even when the reunion seems to have 'failed' or 'be failing' in terms of building a relationship with someone else, it might well be a process from which you can learn most about yourself. The ideal might be to learn a lot about yourself *and* forge a strong relationship with your birth relatives, but you cannot rely on other people to match your hopes and expectations. Rather than expecting to have an ideal or even a 'good' relationship with your birth relative, a more realistic aim might be to find out as much about yourself as you can. Cora, who had met her birth father but been rejected by her birth mother, reviewed her experiences thus:

> **❝**I feel that I'm the person that I am because of the adversity that I've been through. There are lots of things, whether we are adopted or not, that we do or don't know about ourselves and that we only find out about them through living our lives. I understand myself in a different way because of having met my birth father, and I might

understand myself in a different way also if I met my birth mother. But at the moment that's not on the cards. But I don't see the point of going round thinking 'oh well I can't be a complete person without meeting or contacting my natural mother'. I don't think that's the case at all. I've definitely gained more knowledge about myself and in a sense a greater understanding and a much closer relationship with my adoptive parents. Because although it was my journey, they were part of it with me, particularly mum. So, if anything, it's brought us closer together and that's a great plus. And I've gained more information about myself, I don't know whether it's given me a stronger sense of myself – maybe it has in some respects, yes. **99**

It is a struggle to get to the level of understanding that Cora, Wendy, Una and many other people in our study achieved. It takes time, too, and a lot of talking and reflecting. One of the downsides of a book like this is that you might be tempted to measure yourself against what other people have done. Or you might try to get the whole reunion absolutely right by thinking carefully about what everyone needs, trying to be fair and realistic about everyone and everything. But there is likely to be a big difference, especially early on, between how you think you should feel and what your feelings actually allow you to do at that point. Viewed as a rite of passage, the reunion should help your heart to catch up with your head. Be reasonable and realistic before you begin, and don't place too much pressure on yourself.

What will help on this journey?

Below we present three key items that will help you on your reunion journey.

1. Timing

Trust your feelings and take each step when *you* feel ready. You can pause, or keep going if it feels right. Una was one of many in our research who emphasised the importance of 'the right time':

66When it does work out and it all just fits into place you think 'why didn't I do it twenty years ago?' And then you think 'but now's the right time'. I've become a great believer that things happen in their right time and for a reason and you might not know what the reason is at the time, and you might spend twenty years trying to find out what the reason is. But things come when it's right. I mean I got back in contact with my [adoptive] Mum and it's right now. It's better than it's ever been and it wouldn't have happened if we'd stayed together or we'd have come back together earlier. I do believe there are right times for certain things to happen. **99**

2. Preparation

You will need to prepare yourself as much as possible before starting out on this journey. By far the most important thing to do is to work out what your expectations are as these are likely to have a huge impact on how the reunion develops. We recommend that you write down your expectations. This will ensure that you give them some thought and will also make them more concrete. We have included two checklists – for those at the beginning of the journey and those part-way through – with some ideas for the sort of questions it is worth thinking about.

Of course, you may not know quite how you *really* feel until you get started. Even so, the more preparation you can do the better. It will probably help to clarify things if you can talk to a few people. An adoption counsellor is likely to be helpful at this stage. It might also be useful to take another look at some of the reunion stories in this book. Which ones triggered the strongest reaction in you, good and bad? Your reactions may well be a clue to how you are feeling and what you are hoping for.

Once you have written down your expectations, take a good look at them. Are they realistic, or are they catastrophic (predicting a rejection) or anastrophic (expecting a perfect reunion)?

Box 3. **A review checklist for those preparing for a search and/or reunion**

- What has triggered your interest in a search and reunion now?
- What are your expectations and goals?
- How might you achieve them?
- How will you get support to do that?

Box 4. **A review checklist for those on the search and/or reunion journey**

- Why did you come to the search and reunion?
- What were your expectations and goals?
- How many have been achieved?
- Are there any unexpected outcomes?
- What still needs to be done?
- What still needs to be finished – can you finish it or let it go?
- How will you get support to do that?
- When you look back at how you were when you began and see yourself now, how do you feel?

3. Support

Although we have emphasised that this is *your* journey it is likely that you will need plenty of support along the way. Do read as much as you can about reunions, but, above all, make sure you talk to people – do not do this by yourself. Talking to other people is often the best way to work out your feelings before and during a reunion. You will also find that you may need someone to offer reassurance and encouragement, as well as share your excitement and frustrations. The reunion journey is a rite of passage and most rites of passage are painful as well as joyous, as Kim experienced:

> **"**It's a huge life event and I think it can be underestimated what a toll that takes on you, and I think I did underestimate it. I think if people are going to find birth relatives they ought to be warned what a toll it does take and if it doesn't take that toll at the beginning it will take it further down the line. It will come out in some way. I was aware that there would be emotional consequences. I mean even with it going well I thought there would be consequences. I don't think you appreciate when you meet somebody how it's going to come out, or how much. I don't think I was prepared for what happens. I would use the analogy of having a child – you know it's going to be hard at the beginning, but you don't know in what ways, and possibly the ways you anticipate aren't the ways that it happens. **"**

There are three main sources of possible support:

- *Adoption counsellors.* These are specialists working for adoption agencies and social services departments with experience of helping people to prepare for a reunion. They can act as your intermediaries. They are also around to provide for ongoing support and advice as the reunion progresses, for adopted people as well as for birth and adoptive family members.

- *Adoption support groups.* There are now adoption support groups in most areas for adopted people as well as birth and adoptive family members (see the Appendix). The groups are set up to provide support and advice on a self-help basis. They are likely to have a range of people with different backgrounds and different experiences which can be a great way to get a wider perspective on your journey. They can also provide you with support from people who are going through the same process as you.

- *Friends and family.* Your friends and family are likely to be the main source of ongoing support. The reunion is likely to have a major impact on them as well as you, not least because you are likely to be preoccupied or distracted by the reunion itself. They may feel protective and concerned about the impact of the reunion on you and your relationship with them. This is particularly true for adoptive parents but it may also be an issue for your partner if you have one. Try to put aside time from the reunion to make sure you maintain these relationships.

Making reunions work

Adoption reunions can be tough, but they can offer huge rewards. We hope that the experiences of those who have already made the journey help you on your way. We end with some suggestions to help to make your reunion, if you have one, work as well as it can for you.

1. Set out on this journey when you are ready. You will know when it is the right time.

2. All reunions are unique. Find a balance and pace that suits you and your reunion.

3. Work out what you want from, or can give to, the reunion. Be realistic about what you can offer each other and the place in each other's lives.

4. You and your relatives are likely to have to deal with some strong emotions. It will take time, patience and probably compromise to sort them all out. Try to work out *why* people feel or behave the way they do (including you!). Be kind to yourself and others if behaviour is not always perfect.

5. If you can, try to let your adoptive family know about the search and reunion process.

6. Keep communicating with all the people involved. If you feel hurt, excluded, angry or swamped then say so, but gently.

7. You'll need a lot of support from people who might share your excitements and disappointments, act as sounding boards, and from time to time suggest a different view on things.

8. Try to maintain a 'normal' life, especially in the early stages when it is easy to feel overwhelmed.

9. Be prepared to adjust your expectations as time goes on. The chances are that the reunion will have good times as well as bad, like all relationships. Nor are you likely to sail through all challenges in a state of perfect tolerance, compromise and understanding! Get what you can from the search and reunion process. Hang onto the good bits and, when you are ready, discard the bad.

10. Above all, the reunion is about you coming to terms with your past, present and future in whatever way you can.

Appendix: Information on search and reunion in the UK, Ireland, Australia, New Zealand, Canada and the USA

Introduction

In this appendix we provide some of the basic information that you will need to guide you through the mechanics of the search and reunion process. The information includes:

- a summary of the legal rights of both adopted people and birth relatives
- contact details for gaining access to birth certificates and adoption information
- information about contact registers
- details of adoption support groups.

We have included separate sections on England and Wales, Northern Ireland and Scotland as the legal framework is different in each part of the UK. There are also separate sections on the Republic of Ireland, Australia, New Zealand, Canada and the USA. We have included details on these countries as the readership of this book is likely to be wider than the UK alone, and also because some UK readers will have been adopted in or from, or have birth relatives in other countries.

For most organisations we have provided telephone, postal, email and web details, together with a brief description of the services the organisation offers. We have tried to be as detailed as possible, but inevitably we cannot give comprehensive information of all legal systems and adoption groups, however valuable a service they provide. For each country though we have aimed to provide enough information to ensure that you will be able to make a start. All information is correct as of Februrary 2004.

England and Wales

Access to birth records

(A) Adopted people

Once you reach 18 you have a legal right to get a copy of your original birth certificate. If you already know your birth name, all you need to do is obtain a copy of this original birth certificate. You can apply for this via the Family Records Centre in London:

Family Records Centre
1 Myddelton Street, London EC1R 1UW
BMD certs: 0870 243 7788
Other Enquiries: 0208 392 5300
Certificate enquiries: certificate.services@ons.gov.uk
Other enquiries: frc@nationalarchives.gov.uk
Website: http://www.familyrecords.gov.uk/frc

Alternatively, you can now apply online for copies of birth, marriage or death certificates from the General Register Office for England and Wales online ordering service at:

www.col.statistics.gov.uk

If you do not know your original name then you will need to apply for access to your birth records under section 51 of the 1976 Adoption Act[1] through the General Registrar's Office at the Office for National Statistics:

Office for National Statistics
Adoption Section
Smedley Hydro
Trafalgar Road, Southport, Merseyside PR8 2HH
Telephone: 0151 471 4313

You will need to write to the General Registrar explaining that you were adopted, giving your adopted name and your date of birth and they will be able to tie this information up with your original birth details. The Registrar General will not send the identifying information held on your original birth certificate directly to you. Instead, by law, it must be sent to an approved adoption counsellor at an agency of your choice and you will need to make an appointment for 'birth records counselling'. It is up to you which agency to go to. You could use your local social services department to receive this information (look them up under 'Adoption' in the phone book) or the Family Records Centre in London (see above) or the adoption agency that arranged your adoption if you know which one it was. If you receive birth record counselling then you will also get form CA6, which enables you to write to the court where your adoption order was made to find the agency (providing it was not a private adoption) that arranged your adoption. By contacting the agency that arranged your adoption you may be able to obtain any other information they hold about your original family background.

(B) Birth relatives

The Adoption and Children Act 2002 introduced new provisions for birth relatives. Birth relatives (mothers, fathers, siblings, grandparents, uncles and aunts) of a person who

---

[1] Similar provisions will be made under the Adoption and Children Act 2002.

was adopted now have the right to ask an adoption support agency to provide an intermediary service so that the adopted person can be informed of the birth relatives interest and wish for contact. It will then be up to the adopted person to decide how they want to proceed, if at all. No identifying information will be given to birth relatives without the adopted person's express permission.

This major new change, introduced by the Adoption and Children Act 2002, will not be implemented until 2005 but when it does come into force intermediary services will be provided in two phases: the first for birth relatives whose relative was adopted before 12 November 1975 and the second for birth relatives whose relative was adopted after that date.

Search resources/other contact details

Birth, marriage and death certificates in England and Wales

To get a copy of a birth (or marriage or death) certificate you will need to know the full name or names and the approximate date and location of the event, and, if possible, the General Register Office (GRO) reference number for the entry. The GRO reference number consists of the Year, Quarter, Place, Volume and Page Numbers. Knowing the GRO reference number will speed things up and costs less. You can find the reference number by looking at the birth, marriage and death registers. Many local libraries have the registers on microfiche, or you can do your own search at the Family Records Centre in London:

Family Records Centre
1 Myddelton Street, London EC1R 1UW
Enquiries: 0208 392 5300
Other enquiries: frc@nationalarchives.gov.uk
Website: http://www.familyrecords.gov.uk/frc

If you have access to the internet you can now search the entire birth, marriage and death registers between 1837 and 2000 for England and Wales online. The Family Research Link service operates on a (modest) pay per page view basis. The link is:

http://www.1837online.com/

Once you have the GRO reference number, or even if you just have details of names and a year, it is a relatively straightforward process to get a copy of the certificate. You can apply by post, telephone or online from the General Register Office:

General Register Office
PO Box 2, Southport, Merseyside PR8 2JD
Telephone: 0870 243 7788 (orders using the main credit and debit cards)
Certificate enquiries: certificate.services@ons.gov.uk
Online: www.col.statistics.gov.uk (orders using credit and debit cards, but a GRO
    reference will be needed).

or in person at the:

Family Records Centre (part of the General Register Office)
1 Myddelton Street, London EC1R 1UW
Website: http://www.familyrecords.gov.uk/frc

The cost of the certificates varies. Currently, applications online and in person at the FRC cost £7 (provided a correct GRO reference is supplied). Applications by post, phone or fax cost £8.50 with a GRO reference and £11.50 without a GRO reference. There is a much more expensive priority next-day service, otherwise GRO reference certificates should arrive within a week, non-GRO reference certificates take about a fortnight.

Directory enquiries

Apart from the telephone services you can also look up telephone numbers for free on the BT website at

http://www.bt.com/directory-enquiries/

Electoral roll

Local libraries usually keep a copy of their local electoral roll. If you cannot visit the area in person it is worth writing or telephoning to see if they will give you the information. A copy of the electoral roll for all areas of England and Wales is kept at the Official Publication and Social Sciences section of the British Library:

96 Euston Road, London NW1 2DB
Telephone: 0207 412 7677
Website: www.bl.uk/

There are also a growing number of online companies offering electoral roll searches for a fee. Use a search engine such as Google or Altavista to search for 'electoral roll'.

Divorce registers

You can have a search undertaken in the Register of Divorces for a fee of £20. To do so contact:

Principal Registry of the Family Division
First Avenue House
42–49 High Holborn, London WC1V 6NP
Telephone: 0207 947 6000

Probate registers

To get a copy of a will (for a £5 fee, including the search) contact:

The Postal Searches and Copies Department
The Probate Registry
1st Floor, Castle Chambers, Clifford Street, York YO1 9RG
Telephone: 0190 466 6777
Fax: 0190 466 6776

Contact Registers

There are two main Contact Registers covering England and Wales:

The Adoption Contact Register

This is a government register, set up in 1991. Adopted people are registered in Part I and birth relatives in Part II. If there is a match the Registrar General will send the names and addresses of any registered birth relative to the adopted person only. The name and address of the adopted person is not sent to the birth relative – it is left to the adopted person to make contact when there is a match. The Registrar General does not provide an intermediary service as part of the contact register (see section below on other support services for intermediary services). Adopted people will need to know their original pre-adoption name in order to register (see section above on access to birth records). Names registered on the contact register remain there permanently unless a removal is requested. There is a one-off fee to register, currently £15 for adopted people and £30 for birth relatives. Registration forms are available from the General Register Office at:

General Register Office
Adoptions Section
Smedley Hydro
Trafalgar Road, Southport, Merseyside PR8 2HH
Telephone: 0151 471 4830
Email: adoptions@ons.gov.uk (you will need to state if you are an adopted
    person or birth relative)
Website: http://www.statistics.gov.uk/registration/adoptions.asp

NORCAP Contact Register

This large and long-standing register is operated by the voluntary organisation the National Organisation for the Counselling of Adoptees and Parents. Adopted people, adoptive parents and birth relatives can register. Adopted people will need to know their date and place of birth and name of the birth mother, if possible. Birth relatives will need to supply the adopted person's birth name, date and place of birth and other relevant information, such as birth mother's/father's name. The birth relative will also be asked to produce documentary evidence of their relationship to the adopted person such as a birth certificate. Registration costs £10 for adopted people (free for birth relatives) although if a match is made then a full membership fee of £15 will be charged. NORCAP provides an intermediary service. Further information and registration forms can be obtained from:

NORCAP
112 Church Road, Wheatley, Oxfordshire OX33 1LU
Telephone: 0186 587 5000 (Weekdays 10 am–4 pm)
Email: enquiries@norcap.org
Website: http://www.norcap.org.uk/register.html (includes downloadable
    registration form)

Support groups and organisations

(A) Agencies offering post-adoption services (including birth records counselling)

If the adoption was organised through a local authority, or a local authority now holds the records, the best place to find the contact details is through BAAF, the umbrella group of British adoption and fostering organisations. BAAF keeps a large database with details of almost all British adoption agencies. They can be contacted at:

BAAF Adoption and Fostering
Skyline House
200 Union Street, London SE1 0LX
Telephone: 0207 593 2000
Website: http://www.baaf.org.uk/agency_db/index.htm (a searchable database of
    adoption organisations)

The largest voluntary organisations involved with adoption are:

Barnardos
Tanners Lane
Barkingside, Ilford, Essex IG6 1QG
Telephone: 0208 550 8822

Barnardos Cymru
11–15 Columbus Walk, Brigantine Place, Altlantic Wharf, Cardiff CF10 4BZ
Telephone: 0292 049 3387

Catholic Children's Society (Westminster)
73 St Charles Square, London W10 6EJ
Telephone: 0208 969 5305

The Children's Society (formerly Church of England Waifs and Strays)
Post Adoption and Care: Counselling Research Project
91 Queens Road, Peckham, London SE15 2EZ
Telephone: 0207 732 9089

(B) Other agencies and organisations

Post-Adoption Centre
5 Torriano Mews, Torriano Avenue, London NW5 2RZ
Telephone: 0207 284 0555
Email: advice@postadoptioncentre.org.uk
Website: http://www.postadoptioncentre.org.uk/

NORCAP (National Organisation for the Counselling of Adoptees and Parents),
    112 Church Road, Wheatley, Oxfordshire OX33 1LU
Telephone: 0186 587 5000
Website: http://www.norcap.org.uk/register.html

Childlink
10 Lion Yard, Tremadoc Road, London SW4 7NQ
Telephone: 0207 498 1933

Association for Transracially Adopted People (ATRAP)
Unit 35
Kings Exchange, Tileyard, London N7 9AH
Telephone: 0207 619 6220

Talk Adoption (Telephone helpline for people aged under 26 who have a concern about
    adoption) Freephone Tuesday, Wednesday, Thursday and Friday 3 pm to 9 pm
Telephone: 0808 808 1234
Website: www.talkadoption.co.uk

Adoption UK (formerly PPIAS)
Manor Farm
Appletree Road, Chipping Warden, Banbury, Oxfordshire OX17 1LH
Telephone: 0870 770 0450

ISPA: Independent Support Service for People Affected by Adoption
11 Lazenby Crescent (co-ordinator Alison Murray)
Darlington, Co. Durham DL3 9QB
Telephone helpline: 0132 535 0378
10 am to 12 noon weekdays

Natural Parents' Network (a self-help organisation for natural (birth) parents and
    relatives)
11 Green Lane, Garden Suburb, Oldham, Lancashire OL8 3AY
Telephone helpline: 0161 287 8737
Email: administrator@n-p-n.fsnet.co.uk
Website: http://www.n-p-n.fsnet.co.uk/

Northern Ireland

Access to birth records

(A) Adopted people

All adopted people of 18 and over adopted in Northern Ireland are entitled to obtain a copy of the original birth certificate. The first step is to obtain a copy of form ACR14 from:

General Register Office
Oxford House
49–55 Chichester Street, Belfast BT1 4HL
Telephone: 0289 025 2000

Once the form has been completed you will then be required to have an interview with a social worker. The social worker will explain the process and give you the relevant application form to return to the General Register Office in order to obtain a copy of the original birth certificate. You can also ask the social worker (if they have not already done so) to give you the application form to return to the court to obtain the name of the agency that arranged your adoption. Once you have this information you will be able to contact the agency to see if they have any other information about your adoption.

(B) Birth relatives

At present there is no legal right for birth relatives to obtain identifying information about the adopted person. We recommend any birth relative to make contact with the appropriate Northern Ireland adoption organisations to get advice and support, including details of any intermediary services.

Adoption Contact Register

The Adoption Contact Register is operated by the Northern Ireland government. Adopted people aged 18 and over can apply for entry onto Part 1 of the register, birth relatives aged 18 and over can apply for entry onto Part 2. If there is a match the name(s) and address(es) of the birth relative(s) are forwarded to the adopted person only. It is then up to the adopted person to initiate contact. Entry onto the register costs £9.50 for adopted people and £27.50 for birth relatives. Application forms can be obtained from:

General Register Office
Oxford House
49–55 Chichester Street, Belfast BT1 4HL
Telephone: 0289 025 2000

Support groups and organisations

ADOPT – Northern Ireland
VSB
The Peskett Centre, 2/2a Windsor Road, Belfast BT9 7FQ
Telephone: 0289 038 2353

Barnardos Northern Ireland
542–544 Upper Newtownards Road, Belfast BT4 3HE
Telephone: 0289 067 2366

Church of Ireland Adoption Society
Church of Ireland House
61–67 Donegall Street, Belfast BT1 2QH
Telephone: 0289 023 3885
Email: admin@cofiadopt.org.uk
Website: http://www.cofiadopt.org.uk/

Adoption UK (formerly PPIAS)
Manor Farm
Appletree Road, Chipping Warden, Banbury, Oxfordshire OX17 1LH
Telephone: 0870 770 0450

Scotland

Access to birth records

(A) Adopted people

Once you have reached 16 years of age you are entitled to a copy of your original birth certificate. To do so you must contact the General Register Office to obtain a declaration form. The contact details are:

Adoption Unit
The General Register Office for Scotland (GROS)
New Register House, Edinburgh EH1 3YT
Telephone general enquiries: 0131 334 0380
Email: records@gro-scotland.gov.uk
Website: http://www.gro-scotland.gov.uk/

Once the completed form has been received by the General Register Office, a copy of the information will be sent to the chosen adoption agency. You will be required then to attend a meeting with an adoption social worker to talk through the process and your options. After the meeting you will be able to apply to the GRO for a copy of the original birth certificate. You may also be given the name of the agency that arranged the adoption. If so, you can approach the agency to see if they have any information relating to your adoption. Birthlink (see below) also keeps a register of the whereabouts of adoption records, particularly those arranged by local authorities and adoption societies.

(B) Birth relatives

At present there is no legal right for birth relatives to obtain identifying information about the adopted person. We recommend any birth relative to make contact with the appropriate Scottish adoption organisations to get advice and support, including details of any intermediary services.

Adoption Contact Register

The Adoption Contact Register for Scotland (or 'Birthlink' register) is run by the independent Family Care Adoption Society in Edinburgh. The register is open to adopted people aged 16 and over and birth relatives of the adopted person. Birthlink does offer an intermediary service to help make contact where a match has been made. Registration costs £20 although a reduced fee can be possible. Registration forms can be obtained from:

> Birthlink
> Family Care
> 21 Castle Street, Edinburgh EH2 3DN
> Telephone: 0131 225 6441
> Email: acrform@birthlink.org.uk
> Website: www.birthlink.org.uk

Support groups and organisations

The Scottish Adoption Association provides counselling and as well as holding the records of adoptions arranged by themselves, holds those for Edinburgh and Lothian Social Work Department, The Church of Scotland, and The Scottish Episcopal Church. Contact:

> The Scottish Adoption Association
> 2 Commercial Street, Edinburgh EH6 6JA
> Telephone: 0131 553 5060

The Scottish Adoption Advice Service (Barnardos) offers counselling and advice:

> Scottish Adoption Advice Service
> 16 Sandyford Place, Glasgow G3 7BN
> Telephone: 0141 339 0772

Family Care (Birthlink) provides help with searching, adoption counselling, intermediary services. Also maintains Birthlink, the Adoption Contact Register for Scotland.

Birthlink
Family Care
21 Castle Street, Edinburgh EH2 3DN
Telephone: 0131 225 6441
Email: acrform@birthlink.org.uk
Website: www.birthlink.org.uk

Adoption UK (formerly PPIAS)
Manor Farm
Appletree Road, Chipping Warden, Banbury, Oxfordshire OX17 1LH
Telephone: 0870 770 0450

Republic of Ireland

Searching in Ireland is currently a complicated and time-consuming process requiring a lot of detective work simply to get a copy of the original birth certificate. It is possible to search but it is very difficult. Fortunately the Irish government is currently reviewing post-adoption services and new legislation is planned offering rights to information and services for adopted people and birth relatives. For current progress on the legislation see the Department of Health and Children and the Adopted People's Association websites:

http://www.doh.ie/
http://www.adoptionireland.com/

The information given below refers to the current situation.

Access to birth records

The first step for adopted people is to find out which agency arranged the adoption by writing to the Adoption Board at:

The Adoption Board
Shelbourne House
Shelbourne Road, Ballsbridge, Dublin 4, Ireland
Telephone: 35 31 6671392

Then contact the agency to ask for as much 'non-identifying' information as you can. Your task then is to try to identify your original birth entry using the information you have gathered from the Register of Live Births at the General Registrar's Office for Births, Deaths and Marriages. The contact details for the General Registrar's Office are:

The Registrar General
Joyce House
8/11 Lombard Street East, Dublin 2, Ireland
Telephone: 35 31 6711863

For much more detailed advice and information on the process, including 'de facto' and illegal adoptions, see the online search guides for adopted people, birth relatives and at the Adopted People's Association website:

http://www.adoptionireland.com/services/tracingindex.htm

The APA website is also a good starting point for birth relatives who are searching for an adopted person.

Adoption Contact Register

The Irish Adoption Contact Register is operated by the voluntary organisation The Adopted People's Association. The register is for adopted people and birth relatives where one or both has a connection with Ireland. Registration is free. For information contact:

The Adopted People's Association
27 Templeview Green, Clare Hall, Dublin 13, Ireland
Telephone: (01) 867 4033 (usually manned on Mondays and Thursdays from 2 pm
    to 4 pm Irish time. Leave message and phone number at other times).
Email: match@adoptionireland.com
Website: http://www.adoptionireland.com/register/

Support groups and organisations

Advice can be obtained from the following:

Adoption Ireland
The Adopted People's Association
27 Templeview Green, Clare Hall, Dublin 13, Ireland
Telephone information line: (01) 867 4033 (usually manned on Mondays and Thurs-
    days from 2 pm to 4 pm Irish time. Leave message and phone number at other times).
Email: info@adoptionireland.com for all general queries
Website: http://www.adoptionireland.com/ (Excellent website with information on
    legislation, addresses of adoption agencies, guides to searching, information on
    campaigns, etc.)

Barnardos
Adoption Advice Service (Tuesday 2–5 pm and Thursday 10–2 pm)
Christchurch Square, Dublin 8, Ireland
Telephone: (01) 4546388

Mathair Ail (provides a phone helpline and an online support service for natural
    (birth) mothers).
Website: http://groups.msn.com/mathairail

The Natural Parents' Network (self-help group for natural families)
PO Box 6714, Dublin 4, Ireland
Email: naturalparents@indigo.ie
Telephone helpline: Sundays 2 pm to 4 pm only (086) 8530 140

Australia

All the Australian states have different laws and systems. Although some of the details vary, the same principles apply in each state. Here we outline the common process that applies in all states while highlighting the main differences. We also give the contact details for the government agency responsible for post-adoption services in each state so that you can get specific information.

In all Australian states and the Northern Territory, adopted people aged 18 and over can obtain identifying information, including the original birth certificate. In some states adopted people under 18 can obtain non-identifying information.

Birth parents similarly can obtain identifying information about the adopted child aged 18 and over in all states except Victoria. The position of birth fathers not named on the birth certificate, as well as the position of other birth relatives such as siblings, varies state by state. See the contact details below for state-specific details.

Access to information for adopted people and birth parents

Stage 1

The first stage in all states is to apply to the state post-adoption service for identifying information. The process is straightforward and simply involves completing an application form to obtain an authority for the information to be released. Adopted people are able to do this from their 18th birthday and birth parents can apply also once the adopted person reaches 18. In some states this stage simply involves completing and returning the application form, in some (e.g. Northern Territory, Tasmania and Victoria) you will be required to attend for a mandatory interview to explain the process and explore your options. In all states (with the exception of Northern Territory) a fee is charged for the service, although this fee can be reduced or waived in certain circumstances.

Birth parents in Victoria   The main exception to the process described above concerns the position of birth parents in Victoria. Unlike other states birth parents cannot obtain identifying information here. Instead birth parents will receive non-identifying information and, if the birth parent wishes to exchange current information or to make contact with the adopted person, the Department for Human Services will approach the adopted person on the birth parent's behalf (see below for contact details).

To obtain the application form and the authority for the release of identifying information contact the relevant state agency at the address below:

Australian Capital Territory
   The Adoption Information Service, Family Services
   PO Box 1584, Tuggeranong ACT 2901
   Telephone: (02) 6207 1080
   Website: http://www.decs.act.gov.au/services/FamServDevelopArea.htm

New South Wales
  Dept. of Community Services
  PO Box 3485, Parramatta NSW 2124
  Telephone: (02) 8855 4900
  Email: family.information@community.nsw.gov.au
  Website: www.community.nsw.gov.au/adoptions (including downloadable
    application form)

Northern Territiory
  Family and Community Services
  PO Box 40596, Casuarina NT 0811
  Telephone: (08) 8922 7077

Queensland
  Local and Post-Adoptions – Department of Families
  GPO Box 806, Brisbane QLD 4001
  Telephone: (07) 3224 7415
  Website: www.families.qld.gov.au/adoptions

South Australia
  Adoption and Family Information Service of SA
  PO Box 287, Rundle Mall, South Australia 5000
  Telephone: (08) 8207 0060
  Email: adoptions@saugov.sa.gov.au
  Website: http://www.adoptions.sa.gov.au/ (includes downloadable application
    forms)

Tasmania
  Adoption Information Service
  Dept. Community and Health Services
  GPO Box 538, Hobart TAS 7001
  Telephone: (03) 6222 7373
  Email: adoption.services@dchs.tas.gov.au
  Website: http://www.dhhs.tas.gov.au/adoption/index.html

Victoria
  Adoption Information Service
  Department of Human Services
  16/589 Collins Street, Melbourne 3000
  Telephone: (03) 9616 2822

Western Australia
  Department for Community Development
  Post-Adoption Services
  PO Box 6334, East Perth WA 6892
  Telephone: (08) 9222 2555
  FreeCall: 1800 622 258

Stage 2

Once the authority for identifying information has been received the next stage is then to use the authority to access information. This will entitle adopted people to approach the state registrar-general to get a copy of the original birth certificate containing their birth name and the name of their birth mother and possibly birth father. It will entitle eligible birth parents to obtain a copy of the post-adoption birth certificate containing the adopted name of the child and names of the adoptive parents. The authority may entitle you to other information depending on the state, including the information held in the adoption records.

Stage 3

The identifying information obtained in Stage 2 can then be used to undertake a search for the adopted person or birth parent. Most states also operate a Contact Register where both parties may register to signal their willingness to have contact. Some states will offer help in searching and state post-adoption services also typically offer an intermediary service to help with making contact.

Vetoes

Although access to information for adopted people and birth parents is relatively open, all states also have provisions for contact vetoes, and some, for disclosure of identifying information. What this means is that adopted people and birth parents can register a veto stating that they do not want to be contacted or to have identifying information released about them. In some states this means an absolute bar on identifying information being released about the person registering the veto. In other states identifying information will be released but a legally binding undertaking has to be given not to make contact (ACT, NSW, Tasmania, Western Australia). *N.B.* the veto system is being phased out in Western Australia with no new vetoes being placed from 2003 and existing information (but *not* existing contact vetoes) being removed after 2005.

Support groups and organisations

There is currently no cross-Australia adoption agency or support group. Most states have fairly extensive governmental post-adoption services as well as a range of support groups. A full list of the state post-adoption services is listed above and these agencies will also have details of local support agencies. Alternatively 'Jigsaw', based in Western Australia, has a comprehensive listing of local agencies in each state:

Jigsaw
PO Box 403, Subiaco 6904, Western Australia
Telephone: (08) 9388 1922
Email: jigsaw@jigsaw.org.au
Website: http://www.jigsaw.org.au/index.html. (A good comprehensive website)

New Zealand

Access to birth records

(A) Adopted people

Under the Adult Adoption Information Act 1985 it is possible for adopted people to get access to identifying information. Adopted people who are 20 or over can get a copy of the original birth certificate detailing their original birth name, the name(s) of the birth mother and possibly birth father. The certificate can be obtained from the Registrar-General of Births, Deaths and Marriage. The full address to write to is:

Registrar-General of Births, Deaths and Marriages
PO Box 10 526, Wellington, Aotearoa/New Zealand
Website: http://www.dia.govt.nz/diawebsite.nsf/wpg_URL/Services-Births-
    Deaths-and-Marriages-Birth-Certificates-and-Adoption?OpenDocument

You must include in the letter:

- your full (adoptive) name
- your place of birth
- your date of birth
- the full name(s) of your adoptive parents
- your address
- a fee of NZ$15.00.

The Registrar-General will then send you a list of counsellors for you to choose from, unless you nominate a counsellor in your original letter of application. The birth certificate will then be sent to the counsellor, and the counsellor will arrange to meet you. The purpose of meeting the counsellor is to receive the certificate as well as to get 'information, assistance and support' about the process, including how to search for and make contact with a birth parent and intermediary services.

Once you have your original birth certificate you can also check to see if the Department for Child, Youth and Family holds any information about the adoption, i.e. an adoption file. To do this contact the local Child, Youth and Family branch, supplying a copy of the original birth certificate:

The Department of Child, Youth and Family Services
Private Bag 6901, Te Aro, Wellington
Telephone: (04) 917 1100
Email: webadoption@cyf.govt.nz
Website: http://www.cyf.govt.nz/view.cfm?pid=147 (Lists all local branches)

(B) Birth parents

Birth parents (that is birth mothers, and the birth fathers if named in the Department for Child Youth and Family records) seeking information or contact with an adopted person aged 20 or over can ask the Department of Child, Youth and Family to make an approach on their behalf. Birth fathers who were not registered on the original birth certificate must apply to the Registrar-General before applying to Child, Youth and Family at PO Box 10 526, Wellington, New Zealand.

Birth parents should write, giving their full name at the time of the child's birth and the birth date, place and birth names of the child, to:

The Adoption Information and Services Unit
Child, Youth and Family
Private Bag 6901, Marion Square, Wellington

Child, Youth and Family will then check to see if the adopted person has placed a veto (see (C) below). If there is not a veto you will be informed and the Child, Youth and Family will start a search for the adopted person to see if they are willing to have their contact details given to you.

(C) Vetoes

Either adopted people (aged 19 or over) or birth parents (of a child adopted before 1 March 1986) can place a veto on information being released about themselves by writing to the Registrar-General (see above). The veto is in place for periods of 10 years, but can be withdrawn at any point. People considering a veto are encouraged to provide some (non-identifying) information and to give a reason for the veto. They are also offered the opportunity to talk to a counsellor about the veto.

If a veto has been placed by a birth parent, the name of the birth parent will not be included on the original birth certificate issued to the adopted person. If a veto has been placed by an adopted person then the birth relative will not be able to use the contact service offered by Child, Youth and Family, although they will be offered counselling services.

Support groups and organisations

Jigsaw New Zealand
PO Box 28-0376, Remuera, NZ
Telephone: (09) 523 3460

Canada

Access to birth records

Access to information varies substantially by province and territory. There is a wide variation between British Columbia, where adopted people and birth relatives have access to identifying information (subject to veto), and other provinces and territories where adopted people and birth relatives may have to rely on an Adoption Reunion Register. In many provinces and territories there is ongoing pressure to change the system. For up-to-date information about each province and territory contact the appropriate government agency at the address below:

Alberta
Post-Adoption Registry
9th Floor, South Tower
Seventh Street Plaza, 10030 – 107 Street, Edmonton, Alberta T5J 3E4
Telephone: (780) 427 6387
Website: http://www.gov.ab.ca/cs/services/adoptions/par.htm

British Columbia
Adoption Reunion Registry
PO Box 9705, STN PROV GOVT, Victoria, BC V8W 9S1
Telephone: (250) 387 3660
Website: http://adoptionreunion.net/

Manitoba
Post-Adoption Reunion Registry
#201 – 114 Garry Street, Winnipeg, Manitoba R3C 4V5
Telephone: (204) 945 6964

New Brunswick
Post-Adoption Services
PO Box 5100, Fredericton, New Brunswick E3B 5G8
Telephone: (506) 453 2949
Website: http://www.gov.nb.ca/hcs%2Dssc/english/services/fcss/access.htm#10

Newfoundland and Labrador
Post-Adoption Services
Department of Social Services
Box 8700, Confederate Building, St. Johns, Newfoundland A1B 4J6
Telephone: (709) 729 3506

Northwest Territories (and Nunavut)
Department of Health and Social Services
Post-Adoption Services
Department of Social Services
Box 1320, Yellowknife, Northwest Territories X1A 2L9
Telephone: (867) 873 7943
Website: http://www.hlthss.gov.nt.ca/reform/StratPlan/projects/Family.htm

Nova Scotia
  Adoption Disclosure Service Program
  Department of Community Services
  PO Box 696, Halifax, Nova Scotia B3J 2T7
  Telephone: (902) 424 2755
  Website: http://www.gov.ns.ca/coms/adoption.htm

Ontario
  Ministry of Community and Social Services
  Adoption Disclosure Registry
  2 Bloor Street West, 24th Floor, Toronto, Ontario M7A 1E9
  Telephone: (416) 327 4713
  Website: http://www.gov.on.ca/CSS/page/services/adopt.html

Prince Edward Island
  Health and Community Services Agency
  Adoption Disclosure Register
  Box 2000, 16 Garfield St., Charlottetown, P.E.I. C1A 7N8
  Telephone: (902) 368 6511
  Website: http://www.gov.pe.ca/infopei/onelisting.asp?numbers=5191

Quebec
  Centre Jeunesse de Montreal
  Service de l'Adoption
  1001 de Maisonneuve Est, 6e etage, Montreal, Quebec H2L 4R5
  Telephone: (514) 896 3100 or (514) 695 5251

Saskatchewan
  Post-Adoption Registry
  207–2240 Albert Street, Regina, SK S4P 3V7
  Telephone: (306) 787 3654

Yukon
  Department of Health and Social Services
  Government of Yukon
  Box 2703 (H-10), Whitehorse, YT Y1A 2C6
  Telephone: (867) 667 3002

Contact registers

Provinces and territories generally operate a contact register (see contact details above). In addition Parent Finders maintains the Canadian Adoption Reunion Register (see support groups below).

Support groups and organisations

Parent Finders of Canada
19 English Bluff Road, Delta, B.C. V4M 2M4
Telephone: (1604) 948-1069
Email: reunion@dccnet.com
Website: http://www.parentfinders.org/

Canadian Council of Natural Mothers
Website: http://nebula.on.ca/canbmothers/

Triad Canada
Website: http://www.triadcanada.ca/

USA

Access to birth records

Provision for search and reunion in the United States varies considerably by state. Currently only Hawaii and Kansas offer adopted adults of 18 years or older unrestricted access to their birth and adoption information. However, adoption pressure groups continue to campaign to change the system in most states, and some state laws may then have changed by the time you read this book. An excellent starting point for a fully up-to-date guide to the law and search process in each state can be found at the National Adoption Information Clearinghouse (NAIC). The NAIC website has a comprehensive and regularly updated listing of access to adoption records by state. See:

http://naic.acf.hhs.gov/pubs/l_acestx.cfm

The website also has a searchable database 'National Adoption Directory Online' listing, by state, the State Reunion Registry, State Confidential Intermediary Services and Support Groups for Adopted Adults and Birth Relatives. See:

http://naic.acf.hhs.gov/database/nadd/naddsearch.cfm

Contact registers

Details of the contact registers maintained in each state can be found via the NAIC 'National Adoption Directory Online' at:

http://naic.acf.hhs.gov/database/nadd/naddsearch.cfm

In addition, the SOUNDEX international registry covers all the US states as well as other countries. The registry is open to any adopted person of 18 years of age or older, birth parents, siblings and birth relatives as well as adoptive parents of adopted people under

18. If a match occurs then both parties will be notified immediately. Registration is free.

Application forms can be downloaded from the Soundex website at:

http://www.isrr.net/registration.shtml

but have to be returned by post. Alternatively you can obtain a registration form by writing or telephoning:

I.S.S.R.
PO Box 2312, Carson City, Nevada 89702-2312, USA
Telephone (from UK): 00 1 (702) 882-7755
Telephone (from USA): 1 (702) 882-7755

Support Groups and organisations

National Adoption Information Clearinghouse
330 C St., SW Washington, D.C. 20447
Telephone: (888) 251 0075
Email: naic@calib.com
Website: http://www.calib.com/naic/pubs/access.cfm

American Adoption Congress (AAC)
PO Box 42730, Washington, D.C. 20015
Telephone: (202) 483 3399
Website: http://www.americanadoptioncongress.org/

Concerned United Birthparents, Inc.
PO Box 230457, Encinitas, CA 92023
Telephone: 800-822-2777
Website: http://www.cubirthparents.org/

Adoptees Internet Mailing List Web Site
Website: http://www.aiml.org/

Further reading

Numerous books have been written about adoption and search and reunion, and we have selected some of those that we think are the most useful. We have provided all the details that you will need to obtain a copy, together with a short description of the contents unless the title is self-explanatory. The list of books is in five parts:

- Being adopted
- Locating information and birth relatives
- Search and reunion experiences
- Birth mother and father experiences of adoption and reunion
- Adoptive parent experiences of adoption and reunion

Being adopted

Brodzinsky, D., Schechter, M. & Henig, R. (1992) *Being Adopted: The Lifelong Search for Self.* Anchor Books. ISBN 0385414269. [Looks at identity issues for adopted people from childhood to adulthood.]

Lifton, B. & Lifton, J. (2000) *Journey of the Adopted Self: A Quest for Wholeness.* Basic Books. ISBN 0465036759. [Another classic on adopted people and identity.]

Perl, L. & Markham, S. (1999) *'Why Wasn't I told?' Making Sense of the Late Discovery of Adoption.* Post-Adoption Resource Centre, New South Wales. ISBN 0957714505.

Verrier, N. (1991) *The Primal Wound: Understanding the Adopted Child.* London: Gateway. ISBN 0963648004. [A classic book about the birth mother–child connection.]

Locating information and birth relatives

Askin, J. (1998) *Search: A Handbook for Adoptees and Birthparents* (3rd Edition). Oryx Press. ISBN 1573561150. [A very detailed guide to the mechanics of searching in north America, includes material on using the internet that will be of general relevance.]

Stafford, G. (2001) *Where to Find Adoption Records.* BAAF. ISBN 1903699010. [A practical guide to the mechanics of searching in the UK.]

Search and reunion experiences

Bailey, J. & Giddens, L. (2001) *The Adoption Reunion Survival Guide.* New Harbinger Publications. ISBN 1572242280. [A US guide offering valuable advice on the reunion process. Some material is US-specific, but much of the advice on the emotional aspect of reunion applies in all countries.]

Feast, J. & Philpot, T. (2003) *Searching Question: Identity Origins and Adoption.* BAAF. ISBN 1-903699-47-9. [Book and accompanying video of 10 people speaking about adoption and search and reunion.]

Feast, J., Marwood, M., Seabrook, S. & Webb, E. (2002) *Preparing for Reunion: The Experiences from the Adoption Circle* (3rd edition). The Children's Society. ISBN 1899783091. [Advice on the reunion process, including personal stories.]

Howe, D. & Feast, J. (2000) *Adoption Search and Reunion: The Long-term Experience of Adopted Adults.* BAAF. ISBN 189978330X. [Accessible book about a large research study on searchers and non-searchers together with short-term and long-term outcomes.]

Iredale, S. (1997) *Reunions.* The Stationery Office. ISBN 0117021504. [Experiences of 15 people who have had a reunion.]

March, K. (1995) *The Stranger Who Bore Me: Adoptee–Birth Mother Relationship.* University of Toronto Press. ISBN 0802072356.

McColm, M. (1994) *Adoption Reunions: A Book for Adoptees, Birth Parents and Adoptive Families.* Second Story Press. ISBN 0929005414. [Canadian guide, but relevant elsewhere.]

Saffian, S. (1999) *Ithaka: A Daughter's Memories of Being Found.* Delta Books. ISBN 03853345016. [Personal account of reunion.]

Straus, J. (1994) *Birthright.* Penguin. ISBN 0140512950. [US guide for searchers, includes the author's own story as well as good advice on how to handle some of the emotions associated with searching and reunion.]

The experiences of birth mothers and birth fathers

Bouchler, P., Lambert, L. & Trisellotis, J. (1991) *Parting with a Child for Adoption.* BAAF.

Clapton, G. (2003) *Birth Fathers and their Adoption Experiences.* Jessica Kingsley Publishers. ISBN 1-84310-012-6. [Interviews with birth fathers in the UK.]

Collins, P. (1993) *Letter to Louise.* Corgi Books. ISBN 0552137413. [Autobiographical account from a birth mother.]

Howe, D., Sawbridge, P. & Hinings, D. (1998) *Half a Million Women* (new edition). *Post-Adoption Centre.* ISBN 0952919702. [Readable account of the experience of birth mothers.]

Wells, S. (1994) *Within Me, Without Me.* Scarlet Press. ISBN 1857270428. [Testimonies of birth mothers from Australia, New Zealand, USA and UK.]

Adoptive parents and adoptive families

Howe, D. (1996) *Adopters on Adoption.* BAAF. ISBN 1873868324. [Personal stories from adoptive parents starting with initial thoughts about adoption through to supporting adopted children in adulthood.]

Melina, L. (2001) *Raising Adopted Children.* Harper Collins. ISBN 0060957174.

Morris, A. (1999) *The Adoption Experience: Families Who Give Children a Second Chance.* Jessica Kingley Publishers. ISBN 1853027839. [Personal stories of adopters from infants to teenagers.]

Index